WELCOME TO YOUR BOOBS!

YUMI STYNES & DR MELISSA KANG

Art by Jenny Latham

STRIPES PUBLISHING LIMITED
An imprint of the Little Tiger Group
1 Coda Studios, 189 Munster Road,
London SW6 6AW

www.littletiger.co.uk

Originally published in Australia by Hardie Grant Children's Publishing in 2022

First published in Great Britain by Stripes Publishing Limited in 2022
Text copyright © Yumi Stynes & Dr Melissa Kang, 2022
Illustration copyright © Jenny Latham, 2022
Series design copyright © Hardie Grant Children's Publishing, 2022

ISBN: 978-1-78895-446-4

The right of Yumi Stynes and Dr Melissa Kang to be identified as the authors of this work and Jenny Latham to be identified as the illustrator of this work has been asserted by them in accordance with the Copyright, Designs and Patents Act, 1988.

All rights reserved.

A CIP catalogue record for this book is available from the British Library.

This book is sold subject to the condition that it shall not, by way of trade or otherwise, be lent, resold, hired out, or otherwise circulated without the publisher's prior consent in any form of binding or cover other than that in which it is published and without a similar condition, including this condition, being imposed upon the subsequent purchaser.

Printed and bound in China.

MIX
Paper
FSC® C020056

The Forest Stewardship Council® (FSC®) is a global, not-for-profit organization dedicated to the promotion of responsible forest management worldwide. FSC® defines standards based on agreed principles for responsible forest stewardship that are supported by environmental, social, and economic stakeholders.
To learn more, visit www.fsc.org

STP/1800/0458/0422
10 9 8 7 6 5 4 3 2 1

YUMI STYNES & DR MELISSA KANG

Art by Jenny Latham

WELCOME TO YOUR BOOBS!

Little Tiger
LONDON

Contents

INTRODUCTION 1
THE BASICS 4
                PUBERTY BOOBS 10
                BOOB VARIATIONS 16
                BRAS 22
SWIMSUITS, BIKINIS AND BOOBS 60
WHAT'S IN A BOOB? 63
COMMON WORRIES ABOUT BOOBS 67
ALL ABOUT NIPPLES 82

MORE COMMON BOOB WORRIES 90

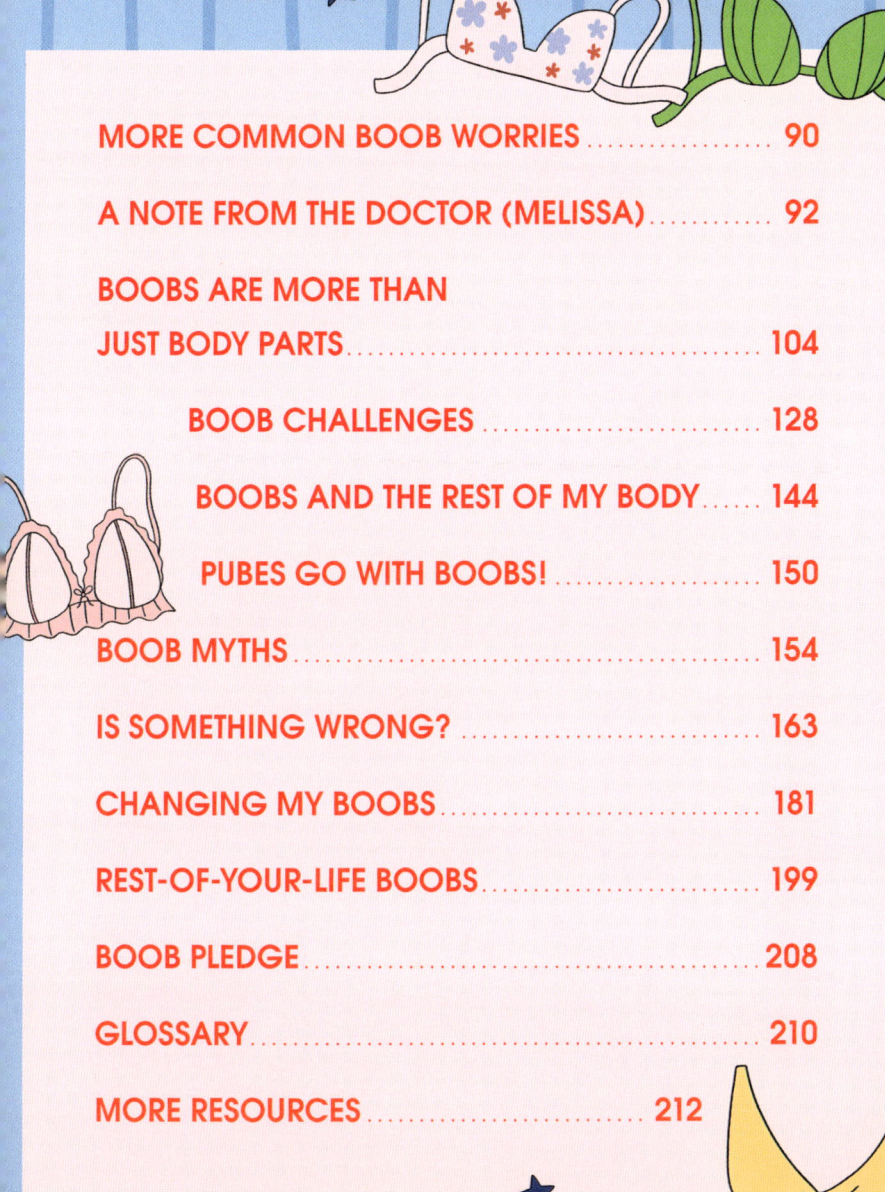

A NOTE FROM THE DOCTOR (MELISSA) 92

BOOBS ARE MORE THAN
JUST BODY PARTS... 104

BOOB CHALLENGES 128

BOOBS AND THE REST OF MY BODY...... 144

PUBES GO WITH BOOBS! 150

BOOB MYTHS 154

IS SOMETHING WRONG? 163

CHANGING MY BOOBS.................................. 181

REST-OF-YOUR-LIFE BOOBS........................... 199

BOOB PLEDGE 208

GLOSSARY.. 210

MORE RESOURCES 212

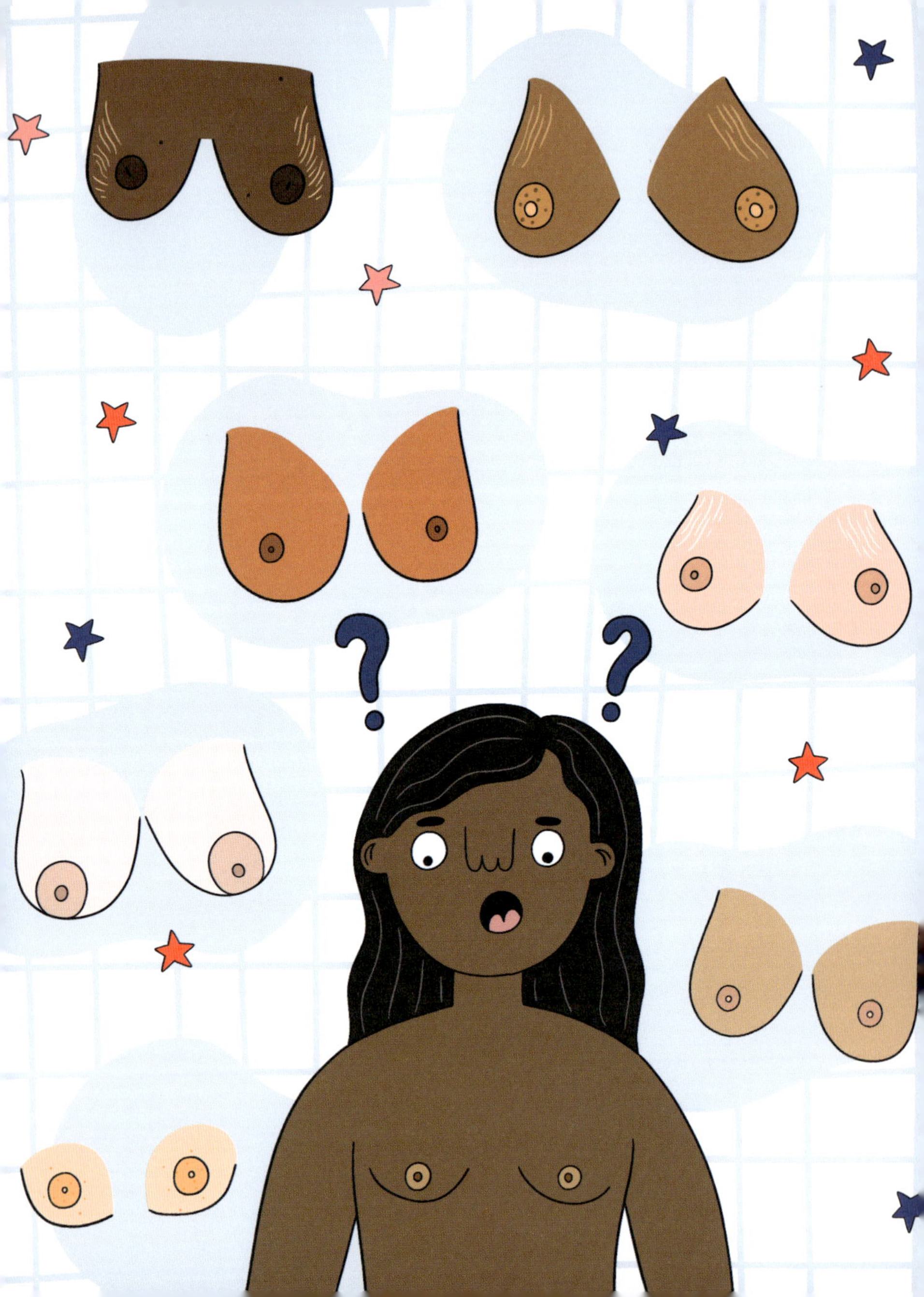

Welcome TO YOUR Boobs!

INTRODUCTION

HELLO, and welcome to our book about breasts – or, as they're often called, boobs!

You might be thinking, 'Hey, it's a bit over the top to have a whole book about boobs. I mean, isn't this like reading a book about … feet? Do we really need a whole book devoted to boobs?'

The answer is: YES!

A LOT of young people have asked us questions about boobs. Like, are my boobs 'normal'? How do I look after them? Why do boobs hurt sometimes? Do you have to wear a bra? (How do you even BUY a bra?) And is it all right to sometimes feel a bit annoyed about the whole boob situation?

Often, these questions start popping up at the start of puberty, when something we never really gave much thought to – our breasts – starts to change and grow on our bodies. Whether we're ready or not.

What you notice as you grow into this phase is that you might have to contend with your boobs in ways you don't with the rest of your body. You have to fit them into your clothes. You have to marshal and support them if they get in the way. You have to deal with throbs and pains and itches. You may suddenly feel quite shy about people seeing them! And, in a fascinating way, you find that boobs have meaning. Just as different cultures can attach different meanings to the clothing you wear, different cultures can attach different meanings to your breasts. Their size, their shape, whether you cover them up or show them off, their very existence!

Just about everyone gets at least some boob growth too, whatever their gender.

AND ALL OF THIS CAN LEAVE NEW BOOB OWNERS WITH A LOT OF QUESTIONS — AND NOT MANY ANSWERS, BECAUSE PEOPLE CAN BE PRETTY SHY WHEN IT COMES TO TALKING ABOUT BOOBS.

But not anymore. We are pulling back the curtain, stripping it ALL THE WAY back, tossing aside the bikini top, and discussing ALL OF IT.

*Yumi and
Dr Melissa xx*

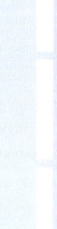

A note about gender and bodies

Just about everyone is born with breast tissue inside them. And as we get older, especially during puberty, breasts can grow in response to specific hormones. These hormones are generally found in greater quantities in girls and women.

Not everyone born with female chromosomes will identify as a girl or woman. Likewise, not everyone born with typically male chromosomes will identify as a boy or man. Others are born with variations in their chromosomes or hormone patterns that may impact on their breast tissue.

In this book, when we use the words **girl**, **woman**, **female**, **boy**, **man** and **male** in relation to how boobs develop, we will usually be referring to a person's sex based on these chromosomes. But we will also talk about people with diverse gender identities and how boobs might affect a person's gender identity.

THE BASICS

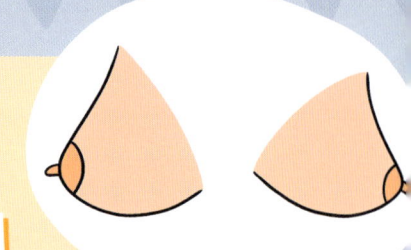

What are boobs?

Also known as **breasts**, boobs generally come in a pair and sit in front of the chest muscles. They are made up of glands, connective tissue, ducts and fat. They come in LOTS of different shapes and sizes. A fully grown breast can look like a small, slightly rounded disc, a wide cone, a fried egg or a round ball (of various sizes), or be bell-shaped.

MORE ON p. 63

Why am *I* getting boobs?

If you're around the age of ten or eleven, then you're probably about to start one of life's great adventures: puberty! Girls start to develop boobs at the beginning of puberty. Your boobs often grow for a couple of years *before* you get your first period.

> My boobs look like someone's been scratching a mosquito bite. *Dee Dee, 16*

> Sometimes boobs get very annoying! In the way! I sometimes miss being a flat-chested kid … but not much. *Cleo, 16*

> If I had to describe a boob to an alien, I'd say it's a female's body part that's round and is stuck on their chest. *Evie, 13*

Who else gets boobs?

Boobs grow most often in girls going through puberty – but that's not the whole story.

Anyone born with breast tissue – that's pretty much everyone – who is under the influence of specific hormones will get boobs!

> I would've been about eleven or twelve, and it was very, very exciting! I remember being OVER THE MOON – I was that kid who wanted to be older than she actually was, so this was a physical marker of me being a big girl. *Lily, 17*

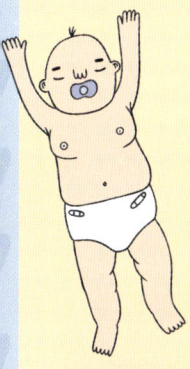

* Newborn babies can have little breast buds for a few weeks which grow because of the influence of their mothers' hormones.

* Most boys going through puberty will have a small amount of boob growth. It usually lasts somewhere between eighteen months and three years. After that, breast tissue shrinks down and the boobs go away.

* Boobs can grow quite a lot larger in pregnant women.

* Medications such as hormone contraception might affect some people's breast tissue, usually making boobs grow a little.

* And some medical conditions can affect boob hormones and therefore make boobs grow or change.

Medical conditions can include certain thyroid problems in women and men, which are relatively more common. In adult and older men, diseases of the liver or kidneys might lead to boob growth. There's a bunch of medications and some rare diseases that might also cause boobs to grow in adult men.

What are boobs for?

Scientifically, breasts are nature's baby-food factory. A teenager's boobs are getting set up for this future possibility. As well as being a tasty, nutritious meal for babies, breastmilk is a natural immunity booster.

For some people, boobs also function as erogenous zones when getting intimate or during sexual contact.

MORE ON p. 160

AN EROGENOUS ZONE IS ANY PART OF THE BODY THAT, WHEN TOUCHED OR STIMULATED, EXCITES SEXUAL FEELINGS.

Are boobs the same as tits?

Yes! Boobs can also be called

kittens, **titties**, **rack**, **cans**, **melons**, **tits**, **jugs**, **baps**, **puppies**, **mammaries**, **bosoms**, **headlights**

and lots of other words.

> I now refer to my boobs as my 'verandah' – like a little porch to catch crumbs and to lean on. *Nelly, 46*

There are so many different words to describe breasts – some are fun, some are silly, some are random and some are kind of offensive. It's up to you which words you use to describe your own breasts, but commonly accepted words that you could use at, say, the doctor's, are **breasts** or **boobs**. It's probably best to stick to those words in front of a teacher or your boss, too – most other slang words for breasts are a bit too funny or casual.

When do boobs start and stop growing?

Boob growth is part of puberty in girls, and for many boys as well. Boobs can start growing when a girl is as young as seven or eight or as old as thirteen or fourteen. They mostly stop growing around one to two years after girls get their first period.

> At school there was like, one other girl, maybe two, who started growing boobs when I did – so I wasn't alone, but we weren't close, so I couldn't really talk to them about it. I talked to my mum about it instead, who was really nice and helped me get through it. *Holly, 15*

That said, it's pretty common for breasts to continue to change in size, shape or contour until your early twenties. By age twenty three, your boobs will have stopped growing, except for during pregnancy or periods of weight gain or loss.

Weight gain can affect boob size throughout your life – if you put weight on in other parts of your body, you can expect to gain weight on your boobs too.

> It kind of felt heavy on my chest when they originally started growing. It was kind of uncomfortable! *Yash, 16*

Are boobs identical twins?

BOOBS ARE ALMOST NEVER SYMMETRICAL.

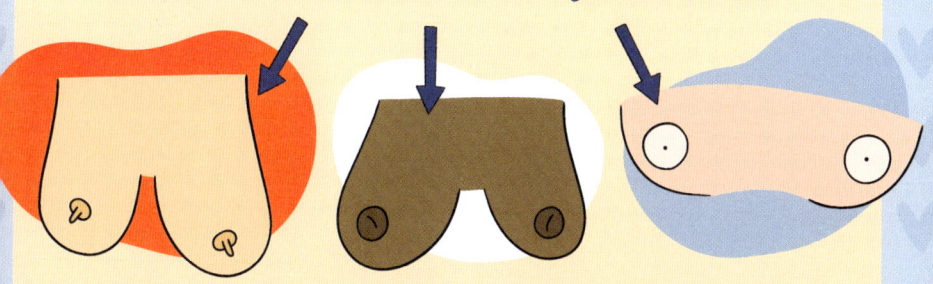

There is usually a nipple in the middle of the roundest or pointiest part of each boob. Nipples can point out or in and are sometimes absent.

Nipples are darker than the surrounding breast skin. You might think the entire darker part is a nipple, but a nipple is just the bit in the middle! The circle around the nipple is called the areola (pronounced A-RE-OH-LUH). The nipple and areola go together on a boob. They might be light or dark brown, pink or red, and they have a different texture to breast skin. On the inside, they are made up of different tissues.

PUBERTY BOOBS

QUESTIONS FOR DR MELISSA

Breast buds: the first sign of puberty

> I don't know if I got buds because I never had a flat chest! I always had a layer of fat so it was hard to tell. *Clem, 39*

> While boobs are developing, is it normal that they start off a bit pointy?

The short answer is that **any** boob shape is normal, at the start, middle or end of puberty.

The earliest sign of puberty in girls is what's called a 'breast bud'. As the name suggests, it means the budding of breast tissue in reaction to the puberty hormones – oestrogen and progesterone.

MORE ON p. 14

> There's a moment when they're growing when they're a little lump under your nipple and it looks like just a big nipple. I was concerned that I might look like that forever. *Dee Dee, 16*

You might be able to feel this 'bud' before you can see it. Suddenly, behind the nipple, there is tissue that wasn't there before! It feels firmer than skin and fatty tissue, but softer than the ribs or chest muscle. It might just be a few millimetres in diameter. If the breast bud is visible, it often looks pointy because it's pushing your nipple out before the rest of the breast tissue has caught up. It might also be more round in shape.

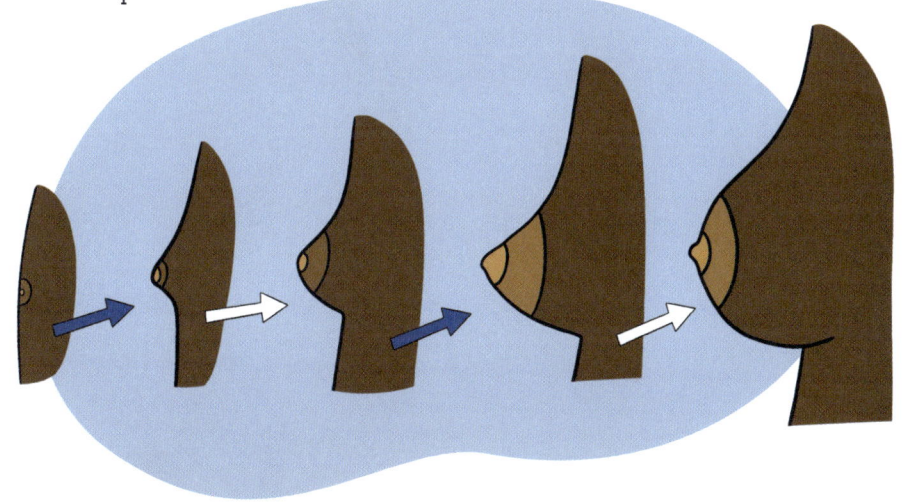

The five stages of boob growth in puberty

Just like growing hair in new places, or getting your period, boob growth is part of the big life change that is puberty!

During puberty, the growth of your breasts can take eighteen months to six years or more. In general, the younger you are when your boobs start developing, the shorter the time it takes for them to go through the five stages of boob development.

Although these five stages might be a bit different in everyone, there is an **overall pattern** that helps you know roughly where you are in puberty.

STAGE 1: Where your boobs are at just before puberty kicks in. You won't be able to see or feel breast buds. Your nipples and areolae (that's plural for areola!) will look the same as they always have.

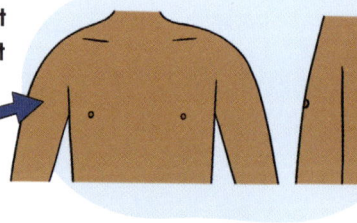

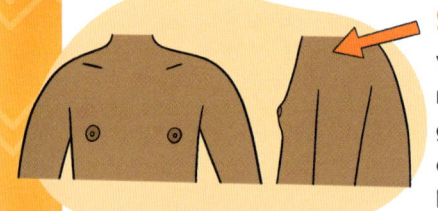

STAGE 2: You can see, or feel, your breast buds. The nipples become more prominent, and the areolae grow bigger. So your boobs are still quite small, but they have a relatively bigger nipple and areola on them.

STAGE 3: Your boobs get steadily bigger overall and take on a rounder shape. Breast tissue, nipples and areolae are all growing in sync together.

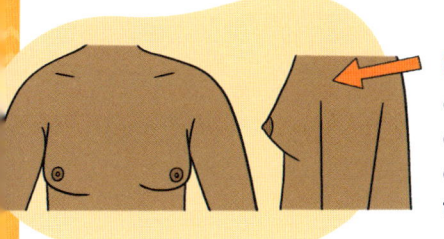

STAGE 4: The nipples and areolae have a little growth spurt of their own, and can look pointy or even like a triangle shape on the tip of a rounder boob.

STAGE 5: The boobs, nipples and areolae have reached their adult size. The nipples and areolae are no longer pointy. Boob shapes can still change over the years, though, and boobs will grow and shrink in size throughout life because of the hormones that influence their growth.

> My boobs went from non-existent to double D's within a six-month period in Year Ten. (I guess I was 14?). I literally remember my friend Kelly saying, 'Where did you get those?!' *Nelly, 46*

> My friends and I don't really talk about boobs and that stuff, we mostly talk about what happens at school. We're not that 'into it' yet. I don't think we're all comfortable talking about it to each other yet. *Grace, 13*

The hormone party

Puberty is like a giant party for many of our body's hormones. A hormone is a chemical messenger that travels through our blood until it reaches its designated stops. It then directs cells and tissues to grow, change or perform a special function. Puberty hormones have an important job to do: they transform our bodies from children's bodies to adult bodies in all sorts of ways, inside and out.

The hormones responsible for boob growth in puberty are called **oestrogen** and **progesterone**. Oestrogen and progesterone levels are much higher in:

- **girls going through puberty than in boys going through puberty**
- **adult women than in adult men**
- **pregnant women than in women who aren't pregnant.**

Oestrogen and progesterone do lots of things, and telling boobs to grow is one of them. It doesn't matter what your sex or gender is – if enough oestrogen or progesterone are circulating, your boobs can grow.

During puberty, oestrogen and progesterone levels go up in everybody. The hormone party kicks off and, over months and years, girls' boobs will grow until they reach adult size and shape.

THE HORMONE PARTY ALSO AFFECTS YOUR MOODS, YOUR BRAIN, YOUR THINKING, EVEN THE WAY YOU SMELL! IT'S QUITE THE PARTY – EVERYONE'S INVITED!

A note about the menstrual cycle (your period)

Other things happen during puberty, like your pubic hair will grow, and you'll get your period. Your period is a monthly 'bleed' that comes out of the vagina and usually lasts around five days. It's a very normal thing that just about everyone with a uterus will experience. The menstrual **cycle** is the whole cycle your body goes through – not just the bleeding part, but the entire time from one period to the next, including all the time when you aren't bleeding. The menstrual cycle starts during puberty, but usually not until boobs have been growing for a couple of years. (Periods are so fascinating and so varied that we have written a whole book about them called **Welcome to Your Period**.)

Periods come up a bit in THIS book because the same hormones that affect your boobs also affect your periods, and there is a link between how your boobs are feeling and where you are in your cycle.

The party doesn't end with puberty!

Once puberty is over, your boobs can still swell up and go back down again during the menstrual cycle, as oestrogen and progesterone levels fluctuate over the month.

Taking oestrogen as a medication in high enough doses will also make boobs grow. This can be prescribed for transwomen who would like to grow boobs.

There are medical conditions as well as some prescription medications that might also make boobs grow, because they have an indirect effect on oestrogen levels in the body.

BOOB VARIATIONS

Like everything in nature and about the body, there is incredible **diversity** in our boobs.

There are very big boobs, very small boobs, and every size in between, and they are all perfectly within what's considered 'normal'. There are women whose boobs grow and stay big after breastfeeding, and women whose boobs shrink and stay smaller after breastfeeding! Genetics play a part too – your adult boob size will depend partly on the genes you have inherited.

It's not that uncommon for people to have an extra nipple (without the breast tissue underneath) or an extra nipple plus boob. Around one or two people in a hundred have more than two nipples or boobs. It's much less common to find the opposite – none or only one nipple, one boob, or one nipple and boob.

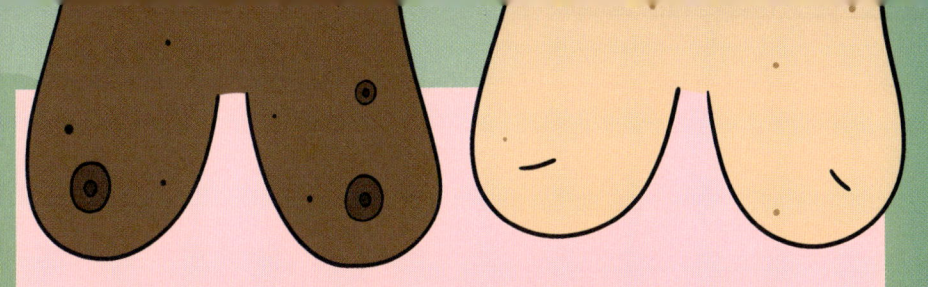

These boob and nipple variations might happen along with other variations in the body. Having more, or fewer, than two boobs or nipples has to do with the way the cells and tissues formed before we were born.

There's lots of variety in the appearance of boobs and nipples, too. Apart from the size and shape of the boob itself, the shape, size and colour of nipples and areolae vary. A common example is what's called an inverted nipple, where it looks like a small dent rather than a point.

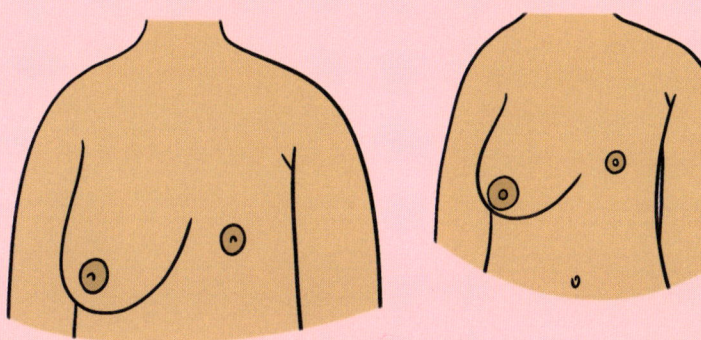

MORE ON p. 86

"My grandmother only grew one boob. So I asked recently and basically she had two but one was very, very small. So I was very paranoid about that happening to me! There was that nagging thing in my head – "Oh man, am I going to grow one boob and not two?" *Lily, 17*

Boobs in my family

Your boobs are going to do what they've been pre-programmed to do genetically. One way you might be able to get a preview of what's going to happen to yours is by checking out and talking to the other women in your family.

> My aunty has huge boobs and I thought I'd end up with her ones but I think I ended up with a nice in-between of hers and my mum's. *Anouk, 18*

SOMETIMES YOU CAN GET A FAIR IDEA OF WHAT'S IN STORE FOR YOU. OTHER TIMES, IT'S TOO RANDOM! YOUR BOOBS MIGHT NOT RESEMBLE THE BOOBS OF ANYONE ELSE YOU'RE RELATED TO.

> My sisters and I are all quite different. I'm most like my mum – my sisters are both teeny tiny and I'm kind of huge now! *Nadia*

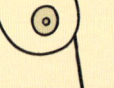

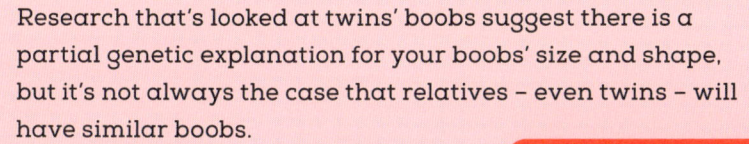

Research that's looked at twins' boobs suggest there is a partial genetic explanation for your boobs' size and shape, but it's not always the case that relatives – even twins – will have similar boobs.

> I was horrified because I've got two older sisters – eight and nine years older than me – and they've got big boobs, and I knew what was probably going to come and that scared me.
> *Berno*

> My sister had big boobs, so there was this expectation that I would have boobs like my sister and I just didn't. *Vicki*

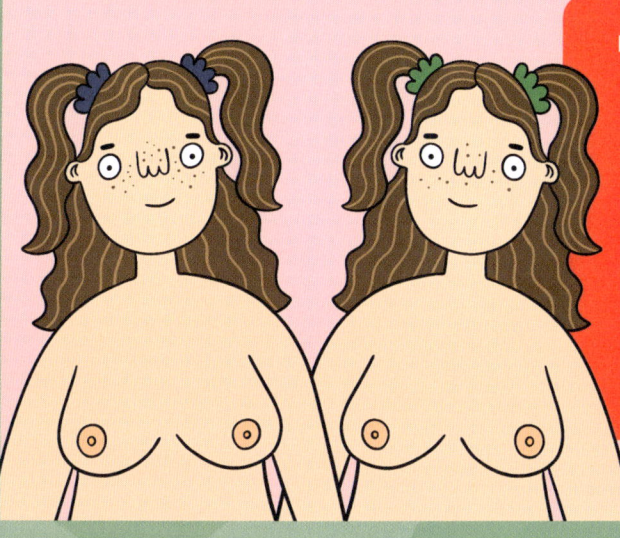

What do other people's boobs look like?

In a lot of cultures, we don't have an opportunity to see other people's boobs. It makes ALL boobs more mysterious – even our own!

If we're lucky, we see our mother's and sister's boobs and maybe those of our close friends. Older family members can be an indicator of what our own boobs may look like in the future.

So because we can't necessarily see boobs in real life, here is a drawing of as many of the different kinds of boobs that exist in real life as we can fit on these pages.

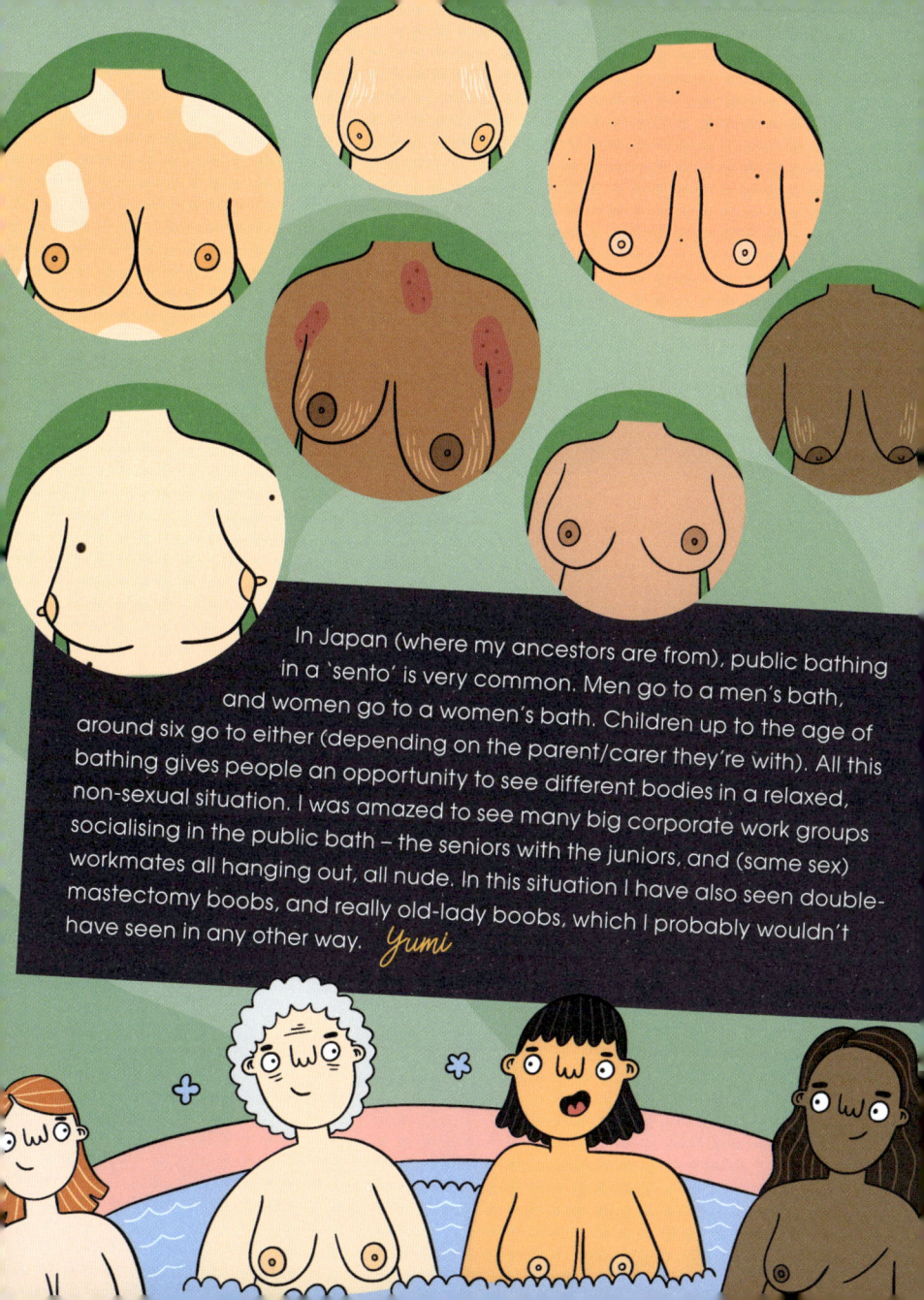

In Japan (where my ancestors are from), public bathing in a 'sento' is very common. Men go to a men's bath, and women go to a women's bath. Children up to the age of around six go to either (depending on the parent/carer they're with). All this bathing gives people an opportunity to see different bodies in a relaxed, non-sexual situation. I was amazed to see many big corporate work groups socialising in the public bath – the seniors with the juniors, and (same sex) workmates all hanging out, all nude. In this situation I have also seen double-mastectomy boobs, and really old-lady boobs, which I probably wouldn't have seen in any other way. *Yumi*

BRAS

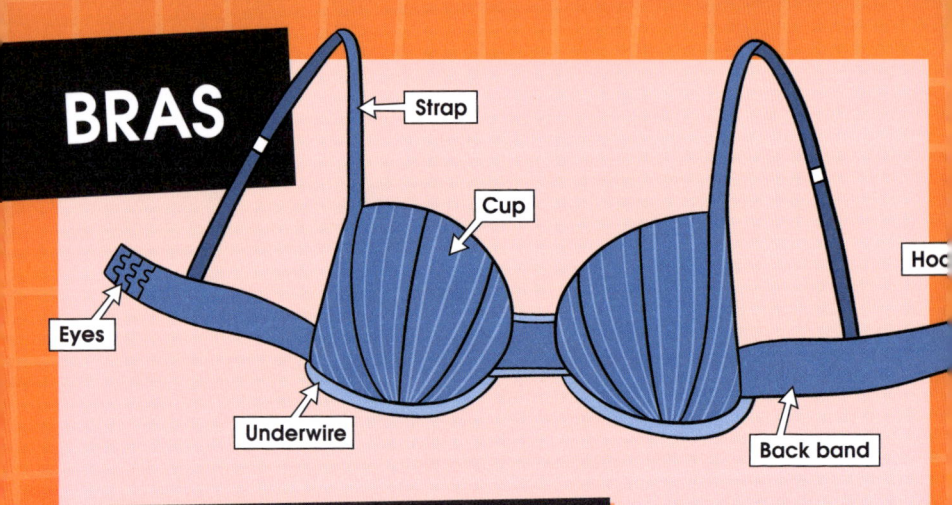

- Strap
- Cup
- Hook
- Eyes
- Underwire
- Back band

Why do people wear bras?

The purpose of a bra is to manipulate boobs in some way – hide them, show them, cover them, reveal them, lift them, support them or modify their appearance. These days people wear a bra to constrain, support and protect their breasts. Stopping 'bounce' is a major consideration, as is appearance.

> I was wearing a bra in Year Six and I remember being mortified because Sarah B snapped my bra and said, "Oh my God, Claire's wearing a bra!" And I wasn't really conscious of it until that moment.
> *Claire, 40*

> The first time my mum was like, "WHAT? You don't need a bra yet! Just wait a few months or years and you'll get boobs soon." She kind of was in denial at the start and I had to ask her a few times. They were there but they weren't that visible and I kind of just wanted to be cool. *Holly, 15*

People haven't always used bras as we know them, though – modern bras were created in the early 19th century and hit the mainstream as a mass-produced undergarment around 1930. Before this, women generally used bodices, camisoles and corsets to shape and contain their boobs to fit with the style of the day.

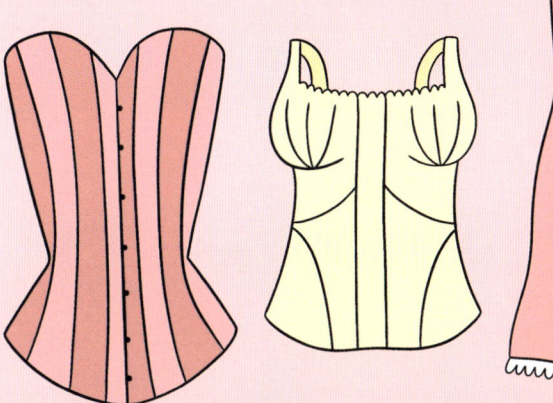

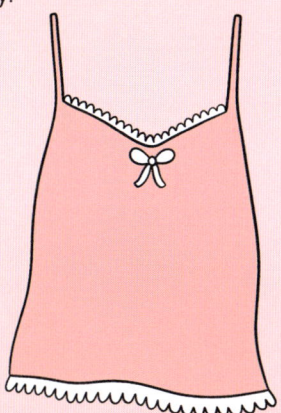

Do *I* have to wear a bra?

Not if you don't want to!

Depending on the way weight is distributed around your body, and the size or shape of your boobs, you might feel more comfortable and supported wearing a bra in daily life. Then again, you might feel perfectly comfy going without one!

> I've stopped wearing bras – not to band practice, not to school! I'm more accepting of my boobs and don't really care what they look like to outsiders, and also? It just feels better. *Anouk, 18*

Wearing a bra is completely up to you.

You might also discover that **other people** prefer it if you wear a bra, but that's not your concern. Your concern is whether **you** feel more comfortable – physically and/or mentally – when you're wearing one.

- Hmmm … when I'm ready.
- I want to run fast.
- Don't need a bra!
- My new bra is my fave.

When my boobs started showing, a lot of people made fun of me for not covering up. Everyone started wearing bras and things and I just didn't. A lot of people would come up and go, "Abigail, I can see your boobs!" And I would go *shrug* "That's fine." *Abigail, 16*

Like clothes in general, we get used to wearing bras and feel more comfortable in them. For most people, though, there is no medical reason to wear a bra. *Dr Melissa*

I once jokingly called bras 'tit prisons' and all these people with much bigger boobs than me explained, 'If you have big boobs, they're "tit supporters"!' and 'No! They are back liberators!' and 'If I don't wear a bra my boobs get in the way and it's painful!' I didn't get it at first, but I got schooled! *Yumi*

What if my boobs aren't big enough for a bra?

You can go without one! However, once you enter puberty, you might find that your breast buds feel sensitive and you'd like an extra layer of fabric between your body and the top you're wearing, even if you don't yet need a bra for support. Crop tops are good for this, as well as so-called 'training bras' (although we prefer the term 'first bras' since boobs don't really need to be trained). Boob tubes or midriff tanks are useful, or you could just use a singlet or a comfy bikini/swimming top.

These are also a good place to start if you know you're growing but are not quite ready to face the bra fitting room yet! Or perhaps you don't want to invest in an expensive bra that might not fit in a few months' time.

I started wearing a crop top in Year Six, mainly because my friends were wearing them, so I thought I'd give it a go. *Gracie N. 14*

At first I was just like, 'OK, I'm starting to get boobs now, what am I going to do? Mum, I need to get some crop tops!' I wasn't really scared to tell my mum because I knew that it was a part of my body and we'd been learning about it in school. *Evie. 13*

I remember not liking it – not wanting another responsibility, like the first time you realize you have to wear socks and shoes when you'd rather go barefoot. *Dee Dee, 16*

To my friends I was like, "GUYS, LOOK I GOT A CROP TOP!" They were like, "OH MY GOD YOU'RE SO LUCKY, I CAN'T WAIT TO GET MINE." *Evie, 13*

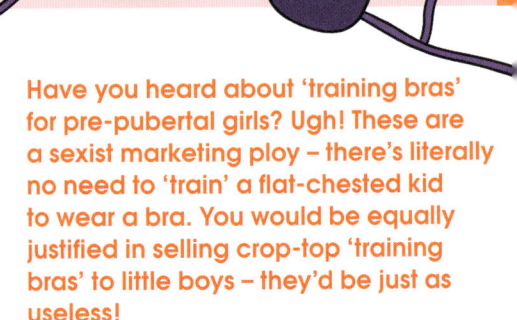

Have you heard about 'training bras' for pre-pubertal girls? Ugh! These are a sexist marketing ploy – there's literally no need to 'train' a flat-chested kid to wear a bra. You would be equally justified in selling crop-top 'training bras' to little boys – they'd be just as useless!

It's fine for a kid to wear a crop-top if they're just playing dress-up and want to have a go at wearing a pretend bra – but they definitely don't need to 'train' for wearing the real thing.

I definitely need a bra! What do I do?

It's time to go bra shopping! Here's what you want to do first:

1 Raising the topic of bra shopping can be painfully awkward. Adults aren't always open to the idea. (They're not keeping as close an eye on your development as you are, and they might not even believe that you need a bra!) Have you got your mum or main carer onboard? Generalizing here, she needs to be part of the process. If not your mum, then your sister, dad or older female friend or relative is usually the best person to ask.

2 Put aside some time for it. Bras, like boobs, come in all different shapes and sizes, so shopping for one can't be done in a rush! Give yourself an hour or so, or maybe even make a whole outing out of it! Lunch, cake, bras? You'll likely try on a few different bras to compare and contrast how they fit, look and make you feel.

> I found it really hard to start the conversation with my mum. I got really nervous! My throat hurt. She didn't really welcome those kinds of chats. I was hugging her one night and tugged on her bra strap a few times then blurted it out – "Mum, I need a bra." *Yumi*

20 Sat 10-11 am Bra Shopping!

3 Pick a place to go bra shopping. Department stores and discount stores are good options as they will carry lots of different brands at different prices. There are also specialty bra and underwear shops. The fancier ones and specialty ones tend to have dedicated 'fitters' who work there and know all about how to find the right size. They don't cost extra – they're part of the service.

4 If you're nervous about being fitted for a bra, you might want to write down some measurements and take them with you to the store. Check out the next section on bra sizes so that you know what to do.

You could also skip the in-store experience by shopping online, but it might take a bit of trial and error. We think it's better to go in person somewhere first so that you can get help if you need it!

GETTING FITTED AT HOME OR FROM AFAR

If you would prefer to be fitted in the quiet and safety of a private home, most big cities have a visiting bra-fitting service. This sometimes suits people who are disabled or neuro-diverse, for example. They come to your home or you go to theirs. You can invite a bunch of friends to share the fitter – make a party out of it! If you live in a remote area, you can still get a good custom fit via Zoom. These fitters are pretty amazing! They were really tested during lockdown and well and truly proved themselves. Usually personal fitters work for a specific brand and take a commission.

The easy way to try on a bra!

Most bras hook up at the back. It can take a bit of practice to do one up on your own, with your hands behind your back. So here's a cheat's method!

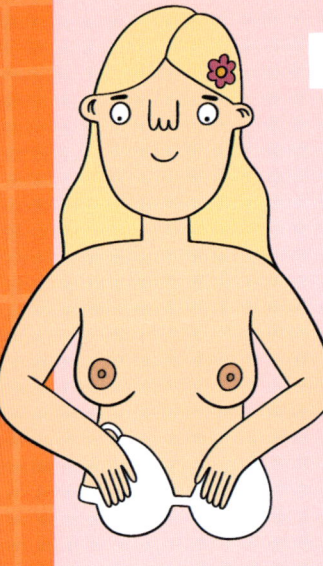

STEP ONE

Wrap the bra around your waist, with the cups against your back and the hooks in front of you at about waist height.

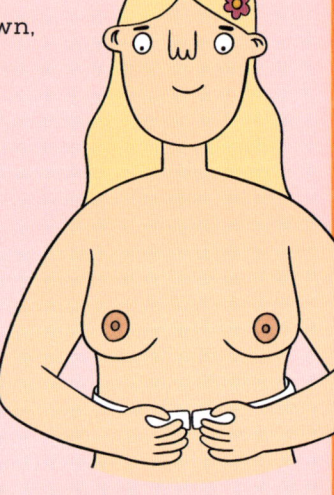

STEP TWO

Hook the bra closed against your tummy, and then spin the bra around until the cups are facing the front.

STEP THREE

Shimmy the bra up, put your arms through the armholes, and then scoop your boobs into the cups.

STEP FOUR

Yippee! The bra is on!

How to buy a bra

MORE ON p. 38

Go to the shop. Try on some bras. Buy a couple that fit. Couldn't be easier – right?

Well, it actually is that easy SOMETIMES – but if you feel nervous about it, that's OK too. Underwear is pretty intimate because it goes on our naked bodies, and that can feel embarrassing. It takes some getting used to. A lot of us go shopping with our mums or aunties if we have them – they act as the voice of experience!

> My advice to younger kids is: everybody goes bra shopping. And no-one is looking at you and thinking that you're weird or strange or awkward! *Lily, 17*

When I first went in I said, "Hi, I'm wondering if I can get fitted?" And she was like, "Yeah yeah!" She guessed that I was an A, and then gave me a whole bunch of sizes to try on and then measured me to see if they'd fit properly. I think she could tell that I was a bit nervous. I was like, 'Do I just go in and put it on?' She was like, 'It's OK, I won't come in while you're trying it on! I'm going to say "Knock knock" at the door.' *Holly, 15*

> Knock Knock!

You should understand that being fitted for a bra properly is TORTURE and your mum is going to pull the curtain aside while you're getting changed and you're going to be like, 'CALM DOWN, MUM' and there'll be people coming in and looking at you and it's THE WORST. But it pays to suffer through it – get it fitted, then get the right bra, and then wear it to death! *Berno*

HOT TIP!

ANYTIME YOU'RE GOING TO TRY STUFF ON AT THE SHOPS (AND THAT INCLUDES BRAS), WEAR CLOTHES THAT ARE QUICK AND EASY TO GET ON AND OFF.

— YUMI

It was an old lady who did the fitting, and she was kind, but it just felt awkward. *Sonja*

Some people don't like touch. Some people don't like undressing in front of you. So it's really about saying, 'How would you like this to go today? I can put the bra on the bed and you can pop it on and then I can come in and look at you.' Some people are really private. *Linda, private bra fitter*

I never use a tape measure. I start with looking at what a girl is wearing and go from there. If she didn't have a bra already I'd make a guess and get a range of sizes. It's as much about comfort and what a girl is comfortable wearing as it is about 'technically' being the right size. *Louise, bra fitter and designer*

If you're going through puberty, and your breasts are growing, you should feel them regularly! You should know if they're getting lumps. If they're bigger. If they're tender. This is a cliche but … they're your breast friend! *Bianca, bra fitter*

A bra fitter in a shop might ask to take some measurements around your chest with a measuring tape, so that they know which size you are. You need to take two kinds of measurements for bras: your **cup size** and your **band size**. More on this in a moment.

Being measured might feel weird, but fitters do it all day, every day – so they're used to it! It actually doesn't have to be awkward. Many fitters are so experienced that they can tell your size just by looking at you.

If you're too shy or nervous to feel comfortable with a fitter – that's OK! If this is the case, it might be a good idea to do the measuring at home before you go in. Write everything down and take it into the shop with you.

How bra sizes work

The short answer is: they kinda don't!

Every bra expert we interviewed for this book said you can get a rough idea of the size that will fit you by using measurements, but it's an imperfect science. Your size in one style or brand of bra might not be the same in another!

Even so, generally bras are made up of two main measurements:

The **band size** or **'back'** measures around your rib cage, UNDER your boobs. You can take this measurement at home if you don't want it to be done in the shop. It's usually a number between 62cm and 150cm – or 24 inches and 60 inches.

The **cup size** of a bra literally refers to the bits of fabric that cup your boobs, and the sizing is measured in letters, starting with AA (the smallest), A, B, C, D, DD, E, F, G and onwards. Again, if you want to take your own measurements before you shop, use a measuring tape to go all the way around your rib cage and meet across your nipples.

Then just search online for 'bra size calculator' to turn these two measurements into your bra size!

IF YOU REALLY WANT TO FIND THE RIGHT BRA, TOSS ASIDE YOUR MEASURING TAPE AND READ ON …

How to find the right bra

Because bra sizes change or fit differently depending on the brand, you might be a 36C reliably in one brand, but a 38B in a different brand. It doesn't mean you've suddenly gained or lost a cup size in one minute – they're just different!

Because every bra fits differently, it's important to try on a few sizes around the size you think you are. For instance, you might be dead-set certain that you are a 34A, but then you try on a 36AA or a 32B and discover it's way more comfortable.

Try on a bunch of different bras before you commit to buying one. Give yourself some time to enjoy it! And also to figure out what kinds of bras you find comfy. As you're about to find out, there are heaps ...

> For the younger clients, they usually balk at honey-coloured bras, thinking, 'That's Nanna!' – but you can't see a honey bra through a school uniform. For someone getting her first 'bra wardrobe', I'd get her one white and one honey-coloured T-shirt bra, and a couple of sports bras, with a little bit of room to grow in the cup.
> *Linda, private bra fitter*

THE PERFECT BRA

A recent study of fashion editors revealed that while many people might own a bunch of bras, they only have one or two that are genuinely comfortable, and they wear those over and over, only washing them every month or two! If you find the 'perfect' bra, it's a good idea to buy another of the exact same kind. So what is the 'perfect' bra? It's one you're comfortable in; the straps shouldn't dig in to or slip off your shoulders, and the band around your rib cage shouldn't feel tight. If there are wires, they should feel like they're on the outside of your boobs, not cutting in. It's also important to get the right bra for the job – for instance, a sports bra should support your boobs so you can exercise without your boobs bouncing around.

> I have eight bras but I only wear two. *Rosa, 13*

> The number-one thing, especially for young women, is that they think they get fitted once and their size will stay the same. While that's true for some women, as you grow and lose weight or gain weight, change your level of fitness, or any change in your hormones, especially conceiving a child, or menopause – your boobs keep changing! It's really important to keep getting fitted to make sure you're getting the right bra support. *Louise, bra fitter and designer*

How to try on a bra

Brand-new bras in shops tend to have the straps set frustratingly short and you'll need to adjust them almost 100 per cent of the time!

It's OK to check that the cup size fits your boobs before you bother fiddling about getting the straps to the right length.

There shouldn't be loads of space between your boob and the cup, and you can check by holding the cup up against the outline of your boob before you adjust the straps.

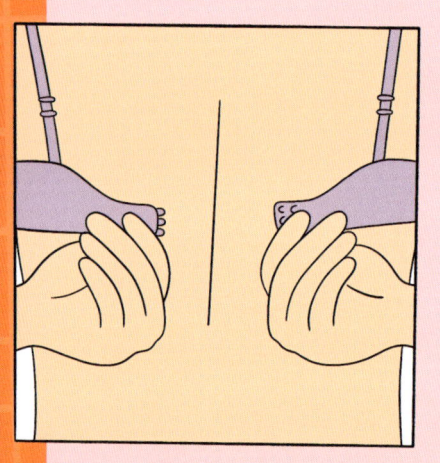

Put your arms in the straps, and pull the bra onto your boobs. Put your arms behind your back, and pull either end of the band together. You should be able to loop the hooks and eyes together. This takes a bit of practice, but gets easier!

The bra will likely have two or three sets of hooks and eyes and it should fit comfortably with the middle or loosest set done up. This is so you can make it a bit looser or tighter depending on what's comfortable on any given day.

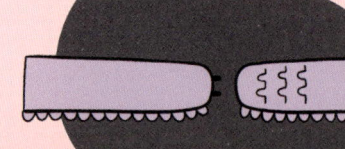

And it allows for the key bit of elastic (the bit that goes all the way around your rib cage) to **stretch** over time – so when it's new you use the looser setting, and once it's stretched you do up the bra on the tightest setting. The band should sit horizontally across your back.

Once the band is done up, you can see how the cups feel on your breast.

Bend forwards and look in at your bust and check if the cup gapes. If you can see into the cup then the cup is too big for you. If your boobs are busting over the sides or top, the cup is too small.

If it's all good, undo the bra and adjust the straps. They should not dig in and you should be able to place a finger between the strap and the shoulder without problems when you are wearing your bra.

It's OK to windmill your arms around and jump up and down in the changing room to see how the bra feels and looks when it's being boogied around in.

BIANCA, BRA FITTER, 30

The average size of bras sold in the UK is 36D, but 80 per cent of people wearing bras use the wrong size. So it's no wonder people sometimes find bras so uncomfortable! Most clients I see for the first time are WAY off their perfect fit.

I would be sceptical if someone measured me with just measuring tape – I don't think it gives the full picture of how unique every pair of breasts are or what style, brand or type of bra suits them. I can measure as a 32DD, but I wear anything from an 30–32 band and E–G cup, depending on the bra. This has changed a LOT as I've gotten older. For instance, many teenagers have full, high-sitting breasts that might be the same bra size as that of their mum. But after aging, weight change or breastfeeding, the shape of your breasts change, so choosing the same bra style as your mum may not work!

Think about it like buying shoes – you need to try them on. No-one's feet are exactly the same, and no-one's breasts are exactly the same. It's trial and error until you are comfortable and supported. Seriously. I have fit twins who have similar breasts, but they hate what the other is trying on! You can't predict what will work until you give it a go.

The number of teenagers who come in and have given up on sport because they're not comfortable in their uniform or they can't find a bra that supports them – it's terrible! So many young people have said to me, "I can't play anymore because I'm not comfortable or I can't run anymore."

Getting a good-fitting bra, especially a sports bra, should be treated like updating your sports shoes – it's essential for so many people.

Different bra types

There are a lot of bras out there – brands and styles and different types! While some of them have specific support structures for particular activities, others are just designed to look a certain way under clothes. Here are some common types:

T-SHIRT BRAS

A T-shirt bra has been specifically designed to be worn under a T-shirt with minimal texture that will show or push through a T-shirt. It has a sponge layer or moulding to hide nipples or any variation in size, and there'll be no seams. It's very smooth, designed to be 'invisible' – an everyday or 'T-shirt' option. The idea is that your silhouette won't draw attention to the fact that you're wearing a bra.

LACY BRAS

Lacy bras, 'non-moulded' or three-part bras are just lace or fabric, or a mix of both in one or two layers. They are probably what we picture in our minds when we hear the word 'bra'. They're usually quite pretty, and often have a bow in the middle and lace around the cup. They're usually for fuller cups, so they're mostly worn by adults. They're also lighter, with not as much bulk as a T-shirt bra. They're also more airy, and good for humid weather.

> If it helps with your confidence, buy something that's pretty! *Cleo, 15*

SPORTS BRAS

Sports bras tend to be the most functional and supportive bras. The idea of a sports bra is that you get maximum support to stop bounce, and that your boobs don't get in the way of physical activity. Bigger-chested people might still like to wear an additional crop-top for extra support, though!

> Over the course of, like, a year, I slowly figured out that because I was a sporty kid and I really hated the fact that I had boobs, I preferred sports bras that were really tight-fitting and didn't show them off as much. *Yash, 16*

MINIMISER BRAS

Minimiser bras are designed for people who want to make their boobs look smaller under their clothes. Different to binders, which are designed to help gender-diverse people or trans boys/men compress their chests to look more 'masculine', minimisers embrace the boob shape, but can reduce the size. They're generally targeted at people with larger boobs. Sometimes people use a tight sports bra to get the minimising effect; from the side, they make your boobs look flat, but from the front your boobs will look wider because they're being squashed against

MORE ON p. 92

your chest. A proper minimiser bra will squash them down without the flesh going out sideways and under the armpit.

Other minimiser bras might be a non-moulded bra with good side support – like a three-part bra with a thick panel at the sides and a fuller cup to bring your boobs forwards, which will make you look smaller front-on.

PUSH-UP BRAS

Push-up bras have padding at the base of the boob designed to 'push up' your boobs to make your cleavage look bigger or closer together. You might choose to wear one if you want to emphasize your cleavage if you're wearing a low-cut garment.

> My friends and I all tend to wear push-up bras so when we're getting changed we'll be like, "OH MY GOD, YOUR BOOBS LOOK REALLY GOOD RIGHT NOW," or "THAT PUSH-UP BRA IS REALLY NICE!" *Evie, 13*

PADDED BRAS

Padded bras have padding in the cups to enhance the size of your bosom, sometimes to sculpt and shape the breasts. They're different to push-up bras in that the padding usually covers the whole boob. There's a scale of padding – it can be as small as the moulding in a T-shirt bra to much more, which will change the boobs' appearance. Many padded bras have removable pads, so if your boobs are different sizes, you can take out one pad on one side to even them up.

STRAPLESS BRAS

Strapless bras are for wearing under strapless gowns, singlets or shoulderless tops, when you don't want your bra to be visible. They have no straps and clasp tightly at the back so you still get a bit of support, padding or coverage.

STICK-ON BRAS

Stick-on bras offer very little support but give coverage and sometimes padding for sheer or challenging outfits.

MATERNITY BRAS

Maternity bras – any bra with a feeding clip in it so you can drop the cup to breastfeed is considered a maternity bra. They can be wire-free or with wires;

if there is wire, it's usually soft plastic wire rather than hard metal, for the mum's sake. It is meant to sit further back behind the breast tissue to try to prevent mastitis. Doctors used to warn breastfeeding mums against wearing a bra with wire. That's changed now; lots of mums might start off as a D cup and then with pregnancy they go up to a G or an H cup and they WANT a wire. The National Childcare Trust says: 'You won't need to ditch your underwired bras while you're pregnant as long as the wire doesn't dig in and as long as it still fits.'

MORE ON p. 174

MASTITIS IS AN INFLAMMATION OF THE BREAST TISSUE CAUSED BY INFECTION. IT MOSTLY AFFECTS PEOPLE WHO ARE BREASTFEEDING.

What is an underwire for?

Most of these bras can come with or without an 'underwire'. An underwire bra has a wire built into it that sits under the breast, against the rib cage, in a crescent shape. They are mostly recommended for people with larger breasts and/or for those who want extra lift. A 'wireless bra' is generally more comfortable than a bra with underwires, but it's also less supportive, so the shape of your boobs will be less structured.

Bras also come in lots of different colours and patterns. Whether you want to go bright, bold or subtle, you'll be able to find a style that suits you!

I use a wheelchair, and when I am shopping for a bra, I often need someone to come with me and help me choose the best one for me. My top priority is to find something that is comfortable and won't need too many adjustments, but I also like to find a bra that is pretty and has a nice design.

When I'm getting dressed, the bra is the hardest garment for me to put on independently. I need help to put a bra on and take it off. I like to wear either a sports bra or a bra with straps that are able to cross over, as this means there is less adjusting that needs to be done, which is difficult for me. In the early days, I tried to wear a standard bra but I found that the straps would fall off my shoulders and sometimes it would undo and I would be wearing the loose bra under my clothes!

While bra shopping is not a difficult task for me, it helps to take something home to try on. I'll return it if it doesn't fit. This is easier than using the fitting rooms in bra shops, especially if I am shopping independently. *Stella*

What is 'cleavage'?

Cleavage is the gap between your boobs. If you have a big bosom and wear a low-cut top, that will expose cleavage. Some breasts are too small to create a cleavage, even with a push-up bra and padding.

Some people think cleavage looks nice. Other people think cleavage is distracting. Ultimately, it doesn't really matter what anyone else thinks – it's up to you if you want to show cleavage!

> In my group, the guys joke and pretend that they have boobs. They push their arms together and make a cleavage and are like, "Oooh, look at my boobs! And it's funny, it makes it not awkward and I really like that. *Yash, 16*

Aren't there lots of rules about which bras go with which clothes?

Kind of.

The commonly held fashion 'rule' that *bra straps shouldn't be seen* gets broken every day. It's a bit outdated now. When it comes to bras, do what feels comfortable for you.

If it helps, there are some informal, common-sense guidelines for which bras work with certain clothes:

A white bra works under a white top, a black bra works under a black top, and 'flesh'-coloured bras work under most circumstances.

The lace on lacy bras will show through T-shirts and other sheer or soft fabrics, and you'll get a less complicated silhouette from a T-shirt bra or sports bra.

The crisscross back of a sports bra usually lines up well with a racerback singlet or 'muscle' tank top for sport.

You won't get much support from a strapless or stick-on bra. They're for 'special occasion' outfits or clothes where you want to look like you're not wearing a bra – but they're not that handy for running around doing stuff!

You don't have to match your bra to your underpants. Some bras and undies come in matching sets, but mostly you can buy (and wear) them separately, or mix and match – the choice is yours!

Comfort should win over looks 100 per cent of the time, so take all this with a grain of salt and just wear what suits you and the way you dress – and what makes you feel invincible, confident and supported.

Why are bras so expensive?

The simple reason bras cost a lot is the work involved in making them. No bra can be completely machine-made and all will have an element of human labour in production. Lace is an expensive material that is

> When I used to wear underwire bras the most expensive bra I owned was about 60 bucks. *Laura*

commonly used in bras, adding to the cost. There's also quite a combo of different materials in every bra: elastic, fabric, metal hooks or clasps, metal underwires, cotton, nylon, silk, lace, etc.

In the UK, at the time of writing, bra prices start at around £6 to £10 and can be as expensive as £100 or more for designer or specialty bras (such as bras for very large cup sizes). Most people can find a good-quality bra for between £15 and £30. If your boobs are larger and growing quite fast you might find you need to upsize more frequently, but the good thing is that with decent care a bra will last you a long time.

> Most of my teenage bras were hand-me-downs from my older sisters. *Yumi*

MORE ON p. 52

BRAS ARE COMPLEX WORKS OF ENGINEERING!

Years of research and development go into the design and manufacture of bras. The makers are trying to create a garment that is light but strong enough to last years. It is expected to support, shape and cover the breast while allowing the skin to breathe, not itch, not smell, and even look good at the same time! A bra is a LOT of work. Like, you don't go to Fashion School and then start making bras after the first week.

Can (and should) I sleep in a bra?

Most people don't sleep in a bra as it can feel uncomfortable, and a bit like you haven't 'clocked off' for the day.

However, sometimes people do choose to wear bras to bed, which is also fine!

> The feeling of taking off your bra at the end of the day? It's the best! It's like when you've had your hair up and then you take it out after a really long time – it's a really good feeling. *Evie, 13*

> One of my friends wears a bra to bed. I didn't feel like it was my place to ask why! She came with us on holiday and I was a bit confused because it's pretty uncomfortable. *Abigail, 16*

I have worn bras to bed since puberty. I feel more comfortable not having them flopping about. I have G-cups. *Rebekah*

I've started doing it because – keeping it real – sleeping on my side with my arms tucked up high means I crush my tits like they're in a vice and I'm starting to worry what they're going to do. *Kirri*

When I have PMS, usually two to three days a month, my boobs feel like being caged! Sometimes they're just BEGGING for support. *Lisa*

I wear a seam-free, super-stretchy, non-wire crop. Just makes me feel a little supported as sometimes without one, my boobs drift to my armpits overnight and I wake up a bit sore. *Jem*

I did when breastfeeding overnight so they didn't get cold! *Lisa*

Bra care

The best way to get the most out of a bra is to wash it by hand. How often you do this is up to you, but you might be surprised by how RARELY people wash their bras! Some people only wash their bras every one or two months. A sports bra should probably go in the wash every time you wear it – especially if you've been wrestling crocodiles, kicking the butts of your enemies, working up a sweat as a world leader, etc. It really depends on what activities you've been doing. If you've been checking your emails while sipping a mocktail in that sports bra, it can probably be worn again!

> **Here are some ways to care for your bra:**

Handwashing

Some people have a small, dedicated bunch of handwashing (including bras) that they do all at once with a bar of laundry soap and a basin or a bucket.

If that sounds like too much work, here's a great hack you can try when you know your bra is due for a handwash: wear it into the shower, soap yourself and your bra down, give it a little wash while it's on, then take it off and finish the wash and rinse while you shower! You can use your body soap for this and it's perfectly fine. It makes the handwashing process less annoying and less time-consuming.

In both settings, target the areas of the bra that need extra cleaning and give the straps, which can sometimes look dirty, and the armpit area, which is sometimes smelly, an extra scrub.

Airing out

Try having two bras on the go – wear one, while leaving the other on a doorknob to air out for twenty four hours. Only wash them when you feel like they have BO (body odour) on them!

Washing machine

To take the best care of your bra when washing it in a washing machine, check what sort of wash is recommended on the tag, or ask when you buy it. Generally you want to use a gentle, cool cycle and a mild soap. You can put your bra and any other delicate underwear inside a 'lingerie bag' or 'laundry bag', which is a simple zippered mesh bag. Then just pop it into the washing machine with the rest of the washing. The bag stops your bra getting bashed around too much during the wash cycle or the hooks catching on material and getting bent out of shape.

> If you don't have a laundry bag, it's just as good to put the bra inside a pillowcase.

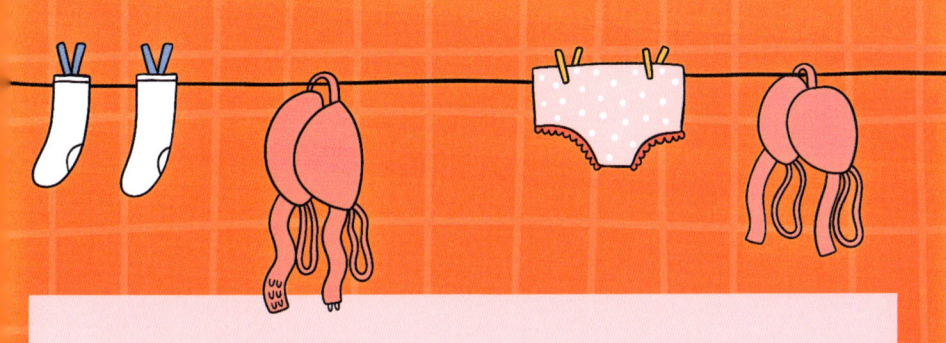

Don't forget to dry

Don't forget that no matter what method you use to WASH your bra, hanging it out to dry immediately is important! If you leave it wet, it can get mildewed, smelly and stale, and even start to rot. (This goes for all clothes, TBH.) Most bras should be dried just by hanging them out – not put in the dryer as it's too rough for such a delicate garment. Sometimes direct sunlight can be too harsh and fade the fabric.

You might need to reshape the cups of some bras, such as padded or push-up bras, when you're hanging them out. Just gently push the cups into the right shape – it's best to do this while they're wet and pliable. This will help them look and feel their best when you next wear them.

> When you hang them on the washing line, hang them with the middle bit on the wire, with both cups hanging down each side and the middle bit draped over the line, and that stops them stretching and going weird shapes or one cup going saggy. *Lily, 17*

I don't have much money

Money gives you choice, and if you don't have much money, this **limits** your choice. It's annoying, especially when the items you need are quite specific in terms of size and fit! If this is your situation, you might need to be a bit strategic and clever about how you find the bras you need.

You still have options – and remember that since the first time the sun rose on the underboob of a teenage kid, people have been in situations where they did not have much money to go bra shopping!

Get your bras second-hand

Keep an eye on what's available in your local charity shops or thrift stores, and sort through hand-me-downs. If you're comfortable, you could put the word out with older people in your family and social circles that you'll accept hand-me-downs, and (this may seem weird!) keep an eye out for anyone a bit older who shares your body type, including – if you're lucky – your bra size! You may be able to set up a long-term relationship with them where their old clothes become your new ones. And it's OK: most people understand that good-quality undergarments are expensive! They're happy to hand them on if they don't need them anymore. In fact, most people will be delighted to know that the bras they don't wear anymore will find a new home.

Improvise

Make do with what you've got! While your boobs are still growing, a singlet or crop top could provide all the support and friction-resistance you need to stay comfy. Bikini tops and other swimwear can do the same job and may be cheaper.

Buy cheap

You can also find pretty good deals at your local discount department or outlet stores. These stores tend NOT to have a free fitting service, so you'll be unassisted when shopping. Cheaper-brand bras may not last as long, but at least they will allow you some time to save up. Even the fanciest stores put their bras on sale at least twice a year, so keep an eye out for those times.

SALE

Make your existing bras last longer by washing them gently by hand.

MORE ON p. 53

Find a charity

As environmental concerns grow and fast fashion becomes a thing of the past, mainstream clothing chains are starting to recycle and repair old clothes. Look out for bra charities in your local area.

> We had no money so my first proper bra was a hand-me-down from my cousin. I was still excited just to have a proper bra! And I was used to having hand-me-down stuff – I liked that it had a little eye clip and was a 'proper' bra. *Laura*

> I have a few hand-me-downs and I have a few of my own, but I haven't really got to the stage of getting ones with padding, I don't really think that I need it that much. *Grace, 13*

DO YOU HAVE BRAS TO SPARE?

If you have too many bras, or bras that no longer fit, look for someone in your life who could benefit from some hand-me-downs and establish the exchange. Againstbreastcancer.org.uk have a bra recycling scheme where they take unwanted bras through a network of bra banks that raise funds for breast cancer research. The bras are also sent to developing countries around the world where bras are too expensive to produce locally through a textile recovery project.

SWIMSUITS, BIKINIS AND BOOBS

Getting into swimsuits can be tricky when your boobs are starting to grow. You can feel self-conscious and like everyone is looking at you. Even if they're not, **this feeling is totally normal**!

> When I went swimming I would always have a towel around me or always wear a full-piece. I only started wearing a bikini this year. I was really self-conscious about my boobs and my body. *Holly, 15*

It's really important that you don't miss out on fun stuff like swimming and mucking around in water just because of your boobs. The best thing you can do is find swimsuits that you feel comfortable in. You don't owe it to anyone to wear a bikini or anything that shows off elements of your body. You don't owe 'prettiness' to anyone. If you're feeling shy about your boobs, look for swimsuits that adds an extra layer of padding around your bosom area so that your nipples and the shape of your boobs are harder to see. Lots of people choose to wear a sun-protective rash vest over their swimsuits for that little

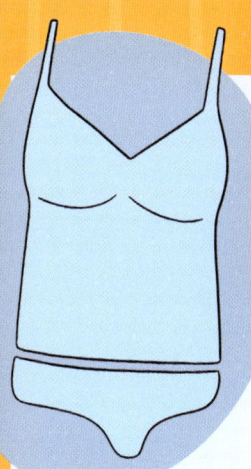

> I grew up doing swimming as my sport so a lot of my swimsuits were chosen for practicality rather than the look of them – like, I had the long ones with the legs! I don't love bikinis because I'm so scared of things falling out – so I have swimsuits that are basically a singlet with a bra thing built in. *Abigail, 16*

bit more privacy. (Oh yeah, and protection from the sun!)

If you're wearing a low-cut one-piece or a skimpy bikini top, you might find that worrying about a boob falling out of your swimsuit ruins your chances of having fun in the surf or the pool. Stuff that! Wear a swimsuit that allows you to frolic freely – without stressing about exposing yourself.

Some people have two sets of swimsuits – one for competitive swimming, surfing or water polo, etc., and one for lounging around in, poolside. The impractical one can be something you work up to (or never use), but the 'having fun' swimsuits need to make you feel confident and secure. There are plenty of cool styles, patterns and colours available that make you feel like a total boss and look awesome.

> We'd all go down to the beach and try to get the boys to look at us. It was excruciating trying to fill my crocheted bikini top – with nothing! *Catharine Lumby*

Boobs affect swimwear hugely – I have to have an underwire situation, otherwise they come out the side, the top, the middle! By having the bikini top on underneath the one-piece, I'm locked in and I'm comfortable and I'm having a lot more fun because I'm not thinking about how they could pop out. *Bernadette*

I remember feeling the need to wear a bikini top underneath a full swimsuit. I grew out of it – but I felt the need to layer up to draw attention away and be more compressed. Aside from sun care, it was to cover up. Especially in that period from age eleven to thirteen. *Cleo, 15*

Wear something that lets you feel like you can swim the way you used to swim when you were a kid. Don't feel the need to wear something to show off in just because that's what other people are doing. *Lily, 17*

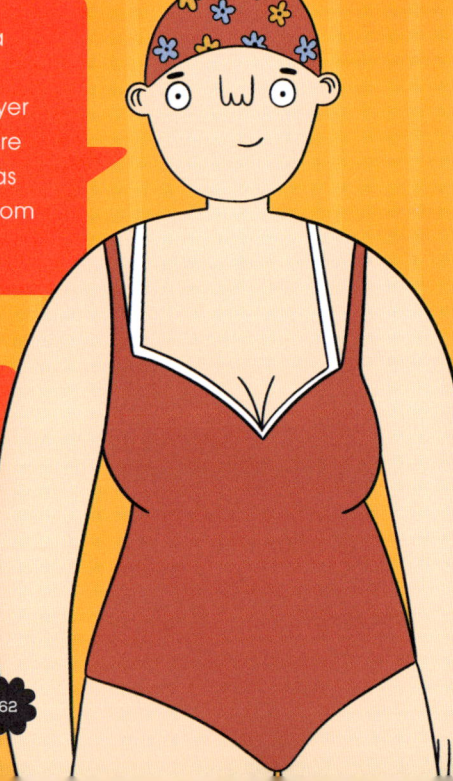

WHAT'S IN A BOOB?

Breast tissue

The inside of a boob is super interesting. For a start, each boob has what's called a 'tail'! You can't see it from the outside, and no, it doesn't wag – it's basically a continuation of the breast tissue up towards the armpit.

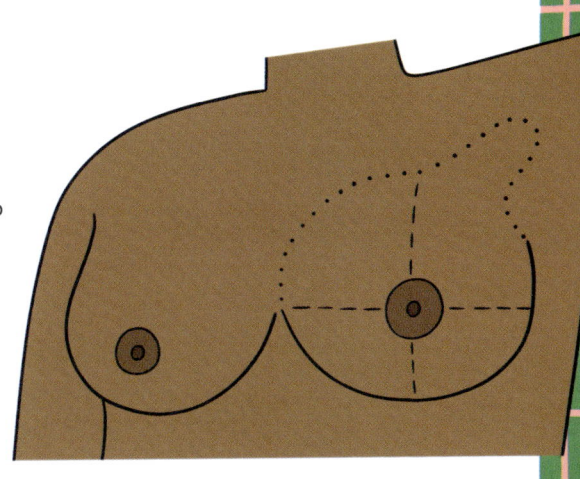

A boob has a mixture of different tissues inside it. There are tissues that produce and transport milk. Other tissues hold the milk-making apparatus together. There is fatty tissue spread throughout the breast and, finally, there are strong bands of tissue that attach all of the above to the chest!

Milk-making cells or 'glands' bunch together like grapes. These bunches, called lobules, are connected to each other by tiny tubes. A group of twenty to forty bunches come together to form a lobe inside the breast. Fifteen to twenty lobes then each have a main tube that connects to the nipple.

To support this incredible collection of glands, tubes and lobes, there's a network of tough fibres called 'connective tissue'. They're like scaffolding holding the breast together. Different people's boobs will have different ratios of all these tissues, giving boobs their own unique texture. This is what makes boobs 'lumpy', 'dense', 'soft' or 'squishy'.

Sometimes lumpy and dense boobs are given the name 'fibrocystic' breasts. This signals that there is a higher proportion of fibre-like tissue and a tendency for glands to swell with fluid and form little sacs ('cysts'). Fibrocystic boobs can feel lumpy and ropy. There is nothing wrong with having fibrocystic boobs – it's just a way of naming what's going on.

- Chest wall
- Ligaments
- Pectoral muscles
- Lobules
- Nipple
- Ducts
- Fatty tissue
- Rib

These inside-boob bits grow and develop fully throughout puberty (see Puberty Boobs on page 10). Before puberty, all that you would see inside a boob are some of the connective tissues and some primitive-looking tubes. The milk-making cells don't start to flourish until puberty hormones hit a certain level.

Nipples

Nipples and their areolae (the darker skin around the nipple) have their own special tissues which are pretty amazing. They're designed to help babies get milk directly from the breast. Inside the nipple part are about ten to twenty tiny tubes that grow during puberty, which is why nipples get bigger, longer and wider. The tubes are designed to carry milk from the milk-making lobules that are deeper inside the breast. The inside linings of these tubes even have tiny muscle-like cells that help 'squirt' milk out.

MORE ON p. 63

Areolae don't have any milk-carrying tubes inside them. They have special glands called **Montgomery glands** that get bigger during puberty. You've probably seen them – they appear around the edge of the areolae as small bumps. They look a bit like goosebumps and are sometimes mistaken for pimples. These glands make a waxy substance that is almost magical in how it works. It cleans the nipple, and lubricates and protects it. The soft wax or oil (which is unnoticeable in most people), also contains an enzyme that kills bacteria!

In combination with sweat glands, the Montgomery glands help to keep your nipples soft and protect them against infection. During breastfeeding they become even more useful (and more noticeable), keeping the area moisturised and disinfected.

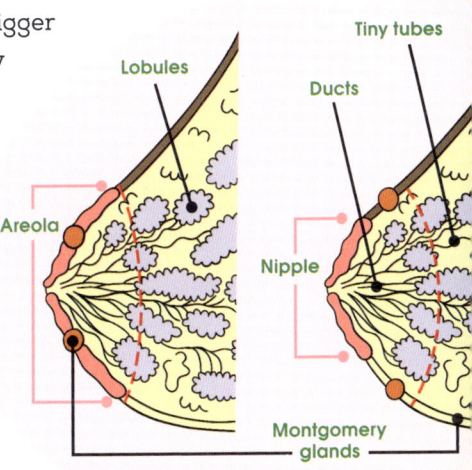

Areolae have a few hair follicles that aren't just for fun! The hair follicles have tiny muscles that pull the nipple up straight to help milk flow. It's these tiny muscles that make a nipple straighten up when it's cold, like a big goosebump!

Nipple tissue also has special nerves that can make nipples very sensitive to physical touch. This sensation can also be increased when the tiny muscles contract. This is why touching nipples can feel sexy and pleasurable. Because the area is so sensitive, touching them can also feel uncomfortable or even painful, especially if they are squeezed too hard, or if you don't want them to be touched. A lot of the time, touching them feels quite neutral.

During breastfeeding, a baby's suck motion stimulates two hormones: one that activates the milk-making tissues, and one that activates the breast to push out the milk (the 'let-down' reflex). This sucking action can feel ticklish, pleasant, uncomfortable, bizarre, neutral or all of the above.

MORE ON p. 200

What holds boobs onto the chest?

The fibres that hold breast tissue together also come together around the breast circle to form bands called **ligaments**. A ligament is a strong, tough tissue that connects two parts in the body. Ligaments usually connect two bones, or bones and cartilage. But boobs have special ligaments called Cooper's ligaments, which literally keep boobs stuck onto the chest!

Cooper's ligaments

COMMON WORRIES ABOUT BOOBS

A lot of advice in this book ends with 'but if you're still worried, go see a doctor'. Maybe you're thinking, 'But I don't HAVE a doctor! And if I have to go see one, my mum will want to know WHY!' On page 140, we talk about what 'going to the doctor' actually involves.

> I used to wear a swimsuit every day for about a year to flatten my boobs because none of my friends had them yet. I just wanted to flatten them and be like my friends. It was really hard going to the toilet wearing a swimsuit every day! I once wore it on a train all the way from Sydney to Brisbane – with a jumper in summer because I thought that would hide them too. *Emma-Jayne*

I'm not ready to deal with boobs yet

A lot of people feel like they want to opt out of boobs. It's common to feel this way as you enter puberty and all the changes start to happen! It doesn't necessarily mean you'll never feel comfortable with them. It might just take a bit of time.

Luckily, the changes are fairly slow. You get time to adjust to having boobs. And, as you go through these years, you may notice that some kids really embrace and show off the changes, and others quite happily go on as if the changes are not happening at all! Sometimes you'll probably forget that you're even getting boobs.

> I still don't like the fact that I have boobs, but it doesn't bother me as much because I know it's OK to feel that way. It doesn't define you or change your personality in any way. *Yash, 16*

If your boobs are arriving and you're not ready to deal with the situation, keep doing what you're doing – wear baggy clothes, tuck your boobs away with crop tops, tight singlets or swimsuits, and face it when you're ready.

> I would wear all the same clothes that I had been wearing all through my childhood so it wasn't apparent – a lot of gender-neutral graphic T-shirts and shorts, NOTHING showy or figure-hugging. *Abigail, 16*

> I feel comfier wearing baggier clothes – I don't wear small singlets that are tight. I like baggier shirts. *Grace, 13*

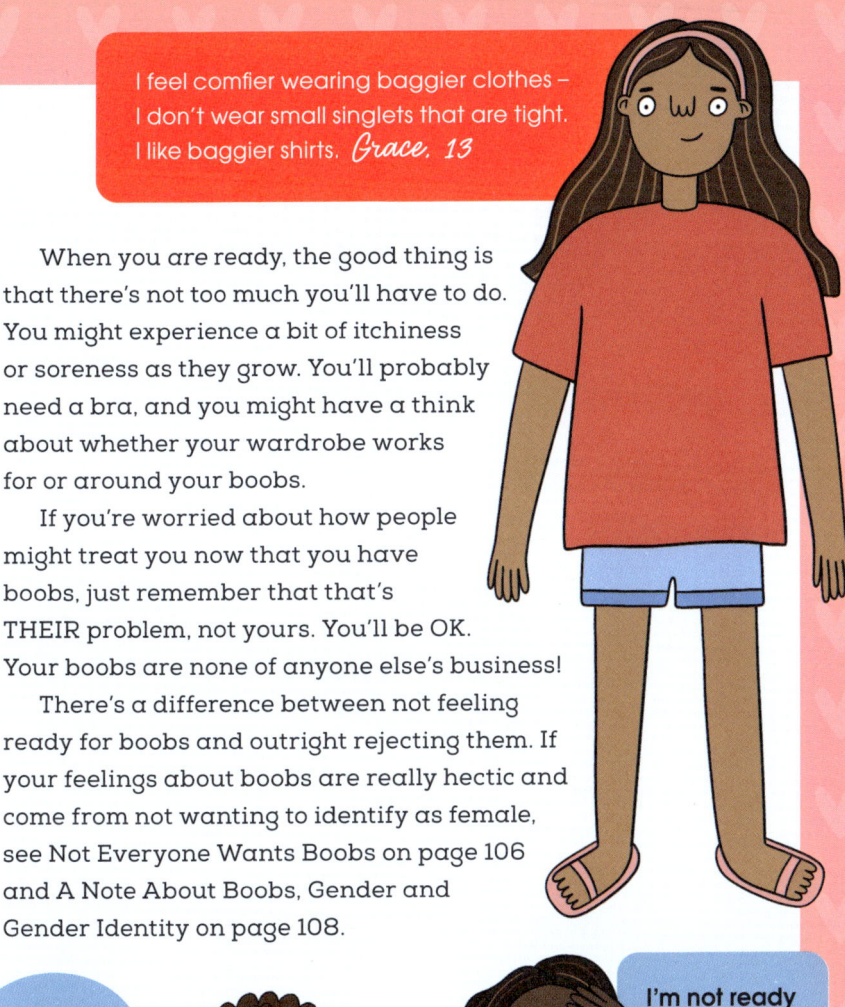

When you are ready, the good thing is that there's not too much you'll have to do. You might experience a bit of itchiness or soreness as they grow. You'll probably need a bra, and you might have a think about whether your wardrobe works for or around your boobs.

If you're worried about how people might treat you now that you have boobs, just remember that that's THEIR problem, not yours. You'll be OK. Your boobs are none of anyone else's business!

There's a difference between not feeling ready for boobs and outright rejecting them. If your feelings about boobs are really hectic and come from not wanting to identify as female, see Not Everyone Wants Boobs on page 106 and A Note About Boobs, Gender and Gender Identity on page 108.

I don't want this …

I'm not ready for this …

My boobs are taking too long to arrive!

> I think probably when I was thirteen they started to grow. But they haven't finished yet. I'm still developing! When will it end? I really have no idea! I don't know – next year I guess I'll just wait and see if anything's happened. *Gracie N. 14*

Watching or waiting for boobs to grow can be exciting for some people, and stressful for others. It can also just be neutral! It changes, too: one week you might be convinced that there's something wrong with your boob growth and the following week you've forgotten all about it.

It's not surprising that plenty of people worry about the way their boobs are growing – when they start, how fast or slow they grow, the way their shape changes, and why they aren't the exact same size.

MORE ON p. 12

We almost never **see** what actual puberty boobs look like. Our frame of reference tends to be adult boobs – we see them on screen, in fashion pages and in ads, as well as in changing rooms at the swimming pool. It's **no wonder** that our own puberty boobs seem different. (Hint: it's **not** because we're swamp creatures.) It's because we're in puberty! And our boobs are a mystery! And it's completely understandable to want to know more about them!

Here are some typical questions I was asked over the many years I wrote for a teen magazine called *Dolly*, where readers sent in questions about anything to do with health, bodies, relationships and feelings. *Dr Melissa*

QUESTIONS FOR DR MELISSA

My boobs are too big or too small!

❝ I'm a five-foot six-inch (1.67m) girl and I feel that my boobs aren't big enough. I know they will grow in their own time but is there any way to speed up the process? Please help if you can? ❞

❝ I have enormous boobs ... and I can never find tops that fit me. They just get in my way!!! I'm a small person but my boobs can't be controlled! Can you help me? ❞

Boobs can start growing when you're as young as seven and as old as fourteen. They can grow quickly (over about eighteen months) or slowly (over six years). Being at either end of this spectrum is really hard for some people, especially if you don't want attention and just want to fit in!

Ultimately, your boobs are pre-programmed to be whatever size and shape your genes tell them to be. We know boob size can cause worry and distress during the teen-ish years. It's true that plenty of people have found ways to change how big or small their boobs look underneath clothes. Padding – with tissues, bits of cloth or bra inserts – can be used to 'bulk' up a bosom. Sports bras and minimiser bras can make boobs look smaller. However, what usually happens is that most people come to accept their boobs and feel fine about them – and that will probably include you. Because they're yours!

> When I was doing ballet in Year Seven, I was about 12 years old and I was the most self-conscious about my chest. We have these things called ballet wraps that are like a tight jumper and at that time I was very self-conscious and felt the need to cover up despite it being very hot and me having these great big sweat marks down my sides! *Cleo, 15*

> I often worry about them not being the right size. I look around at other people in my year and sometimes I get really self-conscious! You know, what if there's something wrong with me? *Amy, 13*

My boobs change shape

Boobs change shape when they're growing, and they differ between people once they're fully grown. Once your periods start, they can also change shape at different times of the menstrual cycle. This is completely normal!

> If I'm on my period, my body doesn't know what to do with itself and everything decides it's going to change size for a couple of weeks. *Lily, 17*

You can change the type of bra you wear at different times of your menstrual cycle. If your boobs become more full just before your period, you can loosen the band by changing where you hook it together. You might also prefer to use a sports bra that's a bit bigger and offers good support.

DAY #1
EYE #1

DAY #4
EYE #4

QUESTIONS FOR DR MELISSA

My boobs are pointy

❝ I'm 13 and I think I have pointy boobs. But the thing is, when I get cold they go round but when it's hot or when it's normal they go pointy. I just want to have normal boobs. Why are they like this?? ❞

Pointy boobs are common in the early and middle stages of boob development. It's actually the nipples and areolae that make them become pointy because, for a while, they grow at a different rate to the breast tissue underneath. It's also the nipples and areolae that react to cold – there are tiny muscles that contract when it's cold and pull the nipple up. However, if boobs are in their pointy phase and the nipple muscles contract, it could actually make the whole breast look rounder.

Pointy boobs don't usually stay pointy for very long. But if it bothers you, you can look for a bra that shapes them more the way you'd like. Sometimes particular styles of bras can make your boobs look more pointy, too. Amazingly, 'bullet' bras used to be all the rage in the 1940s and 1950s – special bras that made your boobs look like cones, missiles or bullets!

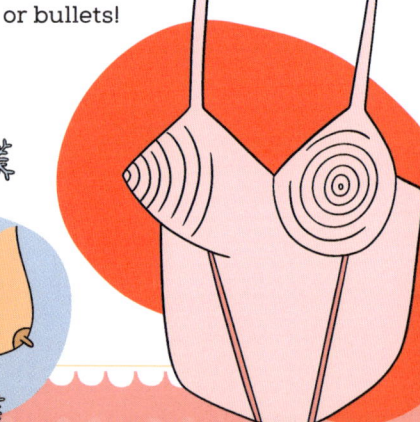

My boobs are different sizes

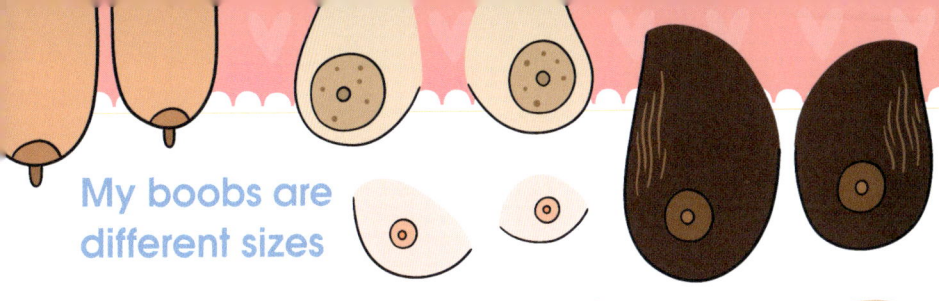

❝ For about the last year I have noticed that my left breast is a size bigger than my other breast. Is there something wrong? I'm too scared to go to the doctor about it. What can I do? ❞

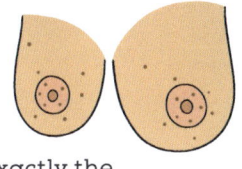

There are lots of body parts that usually come in pairs: hands, feet, eyes, ears and … boobs! It's the same on the inside as well: kidneys, ovaries and testicles, to name a few. None of our paired parts are exactly the same size or shape. Puberty boobs are very likely to be different in size and shape from each other in Stages Two and Three of boob development.

MORE ON p. 12

When I was first growing boobs, they were quite lopsided. They kind of evened out. *Anouk, 18*

I've got one boob bigger than the other – one definitely hangs a little bit lower than the other. I also have got hair on the areola which I never knew other women had until I was in my twenties, and I felt really self-conscious about that! *Clem, 39*

Asymmetry can also affect the nipple and areola, or the way boobs point, or the way they hang on the chest – with one lower than the other. By the time your boobs reach Stage Five, there's usually more evenness, but they are never exactly the same, and a natural difference in size can be almost a full bra-cup size. For what it's worth, it's more common for the left boob to be slightly bigger than the right once they're both fully grown.

So if this is you, all we can say is: don't worry! Boob asymmetry can cause some concern, but it's super common – ESPECIALLY during the 'growing' stage of getting boobs. Most of the time, any size difference between your boobs won't be noticeable to anyone but you. Mostly it will be evened out by wearing a bra. But if it makes you feel more comfortable, you could always use padding on one side to make the size difference less noticeable.

If you're still worried, you can talk to your doctor or school nurse. It might seem mortifying to talk about, but it'll probably be a big relief to have a medical expert tell you everything is normal.

MORE ON p. 141

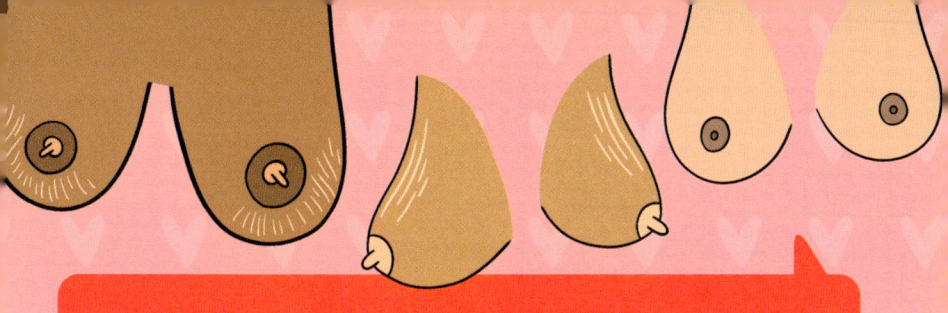

In my breastfeeding advocacy work, I've seen that asymmetrical breasts are incredibly common. As a woman who talks to a lot of people with boobs, the most shocking thing is that everyone thinks they are the only one. Around fifty per cent of women actually have noticeably asymmetrical breasts. It's far more common than people think! *Lauren Elise Threadgate, 35*

DEALING WITH ASYMMETRY

When one boob is MUCH bigger or smaller than the other, bra fitters can accommodate asymmetry – and they do all the time. You get a bra that fits the larger boob, then 'top up' the smaller side with a 'chicken fillet' (a filler that's shaped like a chicken breast fillet) or padding. There are also operations that involve an implant or a breast reduction (mammoplasty), or some combination of both.

MORE ON p. 182 – 187

MEGAN'S EXPERIENCE

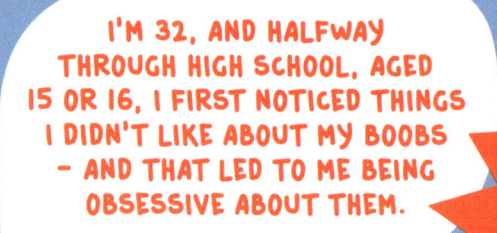

I'M 32, AND HALFWAY THROUGH HIGH SCHOOL, AGED 15 OR 16, I FIRST NOTICED THINGS I DIDN'T LIKE ABOUT MY BOOBS – AND THAT LED TO ME BEING OBSESSIVE ABOUT THEM.

AND OVER THE COURSE OF A FEW MONTHS, I WAS LIKE, HANG ON. THE RIGHT ONE IS BIGGER THAN THE LEFT.

The right one is a C cup and the left is a B cup. The left nipple points forward and the right one pushes out slightly towards the right. I would always choose a push-up style of bra, or a really firm cup, and viewed them as the only kinds of bra that those boobs 'should' be put in – ones that shape breasts into a perfectly symmetrical appearance.

When I started dating, I never enjoyed the experience of people seeing my breasts or touching them. Even though men I've dated have never insulted or judged them. But I have still never talked to my partner about my asymmetrical breasts. I feel a bit silly. It's frivolous, nothing's broken!

I would want young people to be very gentle with themselves. Remember, when you look DOWN at your boobs, it's different to what people are seeing looking straight on at you, through clothes! You might want to 'fix' what you think is wrong with your body, but hey, your body doesn't need fixing. It works beautifully. I've learned to be gentle on myself too.

I've been on both sides! When I was younger I was worried because my boobs were too small, and then by the end of my teens I was buying minimiser bras because they were 'too big'! If I've learned one thing it's that you'll stress a lot *less* by making peace with your body. There's always someone who wishes their boobs were more like yours. *Marisa, 36*

QUESTIONS FOR DR MELISSA

Stripy, stretch-marked boobs

❝ I have stretch marks on my breasts! Is there any way I could get rid of them? ❞

❝ I've got stripes on the side of my bottom and a bit on my boobs. Why are they there? They kind of look like scars. I hope they go away, they're so noticeable when you wear swimsuits. Can you tell me why? ❞

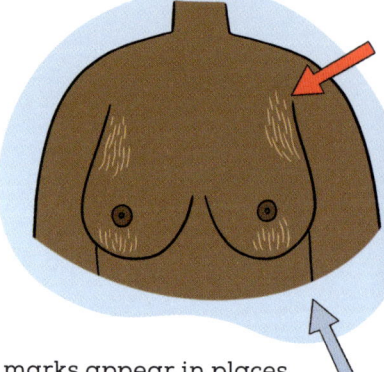

Stretch marks appear in places where skin is stretched as a part of the body grows. Little kids and older adults often get them, but they're **more common in puberty** and during pregnancy, and also more common in girls and women than in guys. In girls, stretch marks can appear on boobs as well as on thighs and buttocks;

80

> When I was a teenager I got red stretch marks around my boobs. They do fade. It took maybe two or three years. Now I have these sheer, glistening marks. None of my girlfriends ever saw them and no boy ever commented on them unless I brought it up – and honestly they don't care. Boys don't care. *Lisa*

in boys they are more common over the upper arms, lower back and outer thighs. Stretch marks look like lines – kind of 'stripy'. They're often pink, white, red or purple and can appear in people of all skin types. Nothing can really get rid of them, but they will fade over time.

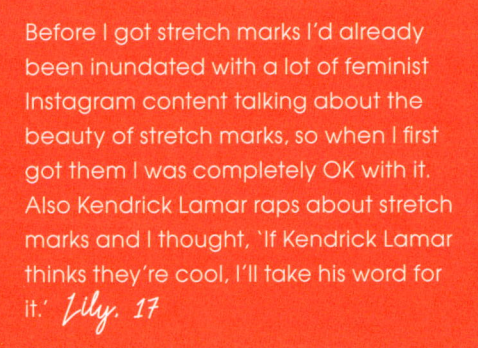

> Before I got stretch marks I'd already been inundated with a lot of feminist Instagram content talking about the beauty of stretch marks, so when I first got them I was completely OK with it. Also Kendrick Lamar raps about stretch marks and I thought, 'If Kendrick Lamar thinks they're cool, I'll take his word for it.' *Lily, 17*

ALL ABOUT NIPPLES

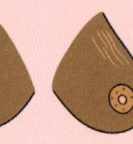

Nipples easily cause as much worry as boob size and shape. You wouldn't be the first person to worry about their size, shape and asymmetry.

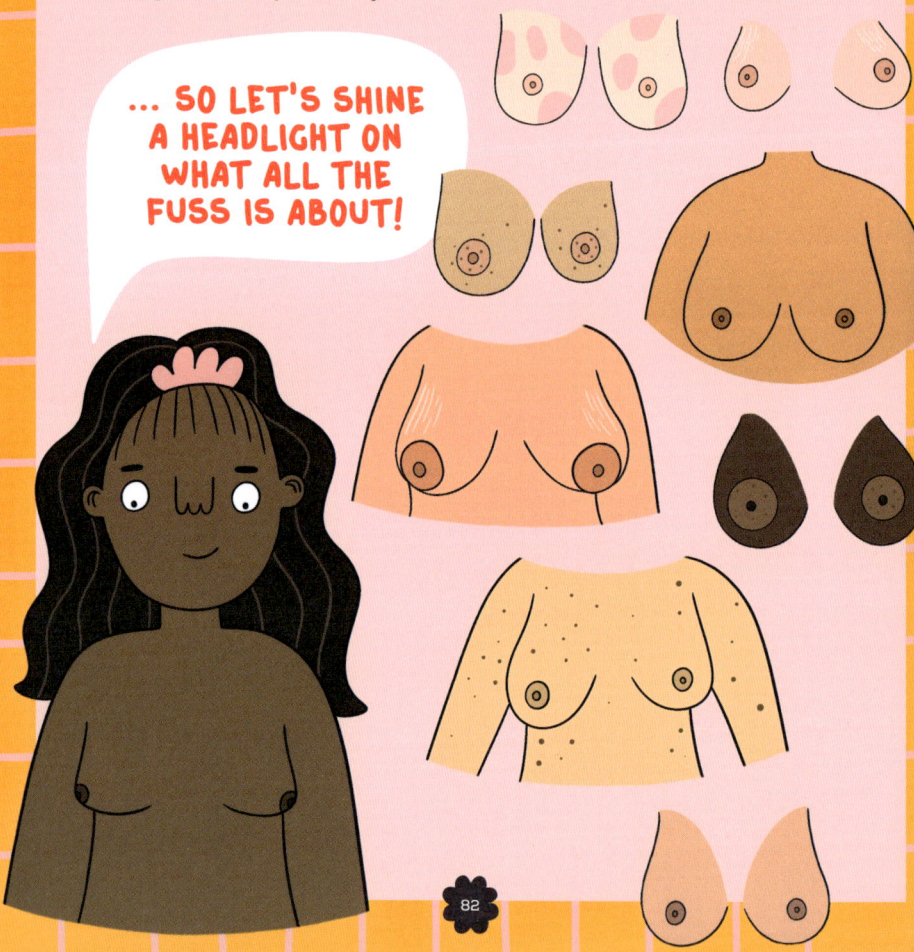

... SO LET'S SHINE A HEADLIGHT ON WHAT ALL THE FUSS IS ABOUT!

QUESTIONS FOR DR MELISSA

What's going on with erect or wrinkly nipples?

> **Um, my breasts are OK it's just first my nipples are soft and then they are all wrinkly and hard. Is this something to do with growing up or is something wrong and I don't want to see a doctor.** – *Anonymous Dolly Doctor question*

MORE ON p. 65

In the areolae, there are special sweat glands next to hair follicles that have tiny muscles attached to them. The muscles contract when it's cold, or when the nipple is touched, making the nipple 'erect'. It's a similar physical reaction to getting goosebumps. They also tighten when you are 'turned on' or getting a 'shivers' reaction. The combination of glands under the skin and the tightening or relaxing of muscles changes the appearance of the nipples constantly, making them smooth or wrinkly, soft or hard.

What you're seeing when your nipples become erect (and usually more wrinkly in the areolae at the same time) is perfectly normal, and indicates your body is reacting to its environment.

MORE ON p. 146

Some people call erect nipples 'having your headlights on high beam'. *Yumi*

When it's super cold, and I suddenly get cold, the areolae would all bunch up and be excruciating! *Berno*

Nipple size, colour, shape

❝ One of my nipples is a lot bigger than the other one. Is this normal or should I see the doctor? ❞

❝ I looked in the mirror the other day and I noticed that one of my nipples is much larger than the other ... like the circle was heaps bigger. What can I do to fix this? ❞

Just as there's variety in boob size, shape and symmetry, so there is in the nipple and areola. Some people have bigger nipples or areolae, some have smaller – but it's all pretty normal!

MORE ON p. 12

Nipples and areolae also go through the five stages of breast development and change their shape and colour along the way. In Stages Two and Four of development, the areola and nipple are more prominent. They will darken during puberty, too.

MORE ON p. 199

Nipples tend to change over time as well, especially with pregnancy and breastfeeding.

My nipples expanded when I had kids (they were much smaller before). I'm Iranian and my nipples are quite brown. *Nadia*

My friends used to make fun of my areolae by pretending to be a DJ spinning discs because they're wide, like records. *Katie*

The colour of nipples is one of those things that most girls I know don't get neurotic about: they just accept it. *Naoko*

QUESTIONS FOR DR MELISSA

Nipple hair

Sometimes I pluck it, sometimes I leave it. *Clem. 39*

> **I'm 12 and realize my nipples are growing pubic hair on them, is this normal?!**

The nipple and the dark circle around it (the areola) go together and grow together. Technically, it's the areola (not the actual nipple) that grows hair and, yes, it's similar in texture to pubic hair for some people. The areola has a few (not many) hair follicles in its skin. It's normal for pubic-like hair to grow from these once your body starts going through puberty. It's safe to gently pluck these using tweezers if you want to, or you can just leave them to grow. Gentle plucking will remove the hair without damaging the rest of the hair follicle (which has the tiny muscle).

MORE ON p. 64

> I was getting lasered and saw on their price list that they did laser hair removal on the areola. And I said, 'What? Do you actually do laser hair removal on NIPPLES? You mean – there are other women out there LIKE ME??' And to me that was a revelation that I wasn't the only person in the world with random nipple hair. *Lisa*

QUESTIONS FOR DR MELISSA

Inverted and split nipples

❝ **I think one of my nipples is inverted. Is there some way I can make my nipple normal? I'm too embarrassed to go to a doctor or tell anyone. I am 14.** ❞

It's fairly common across genders to be born with one or both nipples that point in instead of out. It's considered a normal boob variation – one of many! Puberty boob and nipple development can also cause nipples to become 'inverted'. This happens when the tiny tubes inside the nipple are relatively short while the boob is growing, but eventually the tubes and the whole nipple grow longer and it points out again.

Some people have nipples that stay inverted (or 'retracted') for their whole lives. Most of the time this does not affect breastfeeding. Often the nipple can be stimulated to stick out, then it will retract again. If one or both nipples inverts in adulthood, it's best to get it checked by a doctor.

MORE ON p. 16

> **Well, lately one of my nipples has split into two. What do I do, should I tell my mum or go to a doctor??? HELP!!!!**

During puberty, what might have once seemed like an 'outie' nipple doesn't stay pointing out. Again, this is because the tiny tubes inside the nipple are short and haven't caught up with the rest of the boob's growth. In some cases, the nipple disappears into an 'innie'. For others it partly points in and **looks like it's split**, or slit-like. The majority of inverted or 'slit-like' nipples point outwards again when puberty is finished or during pregnancy or when breastfeeding. If this is you, don't freak out! It's perfectly normal and will pass with time.

If you still have worries, though, it's best to go see your doctor. It might be embarrassing, but they deal with this sort of thing all the time and can help put your mind at ease!

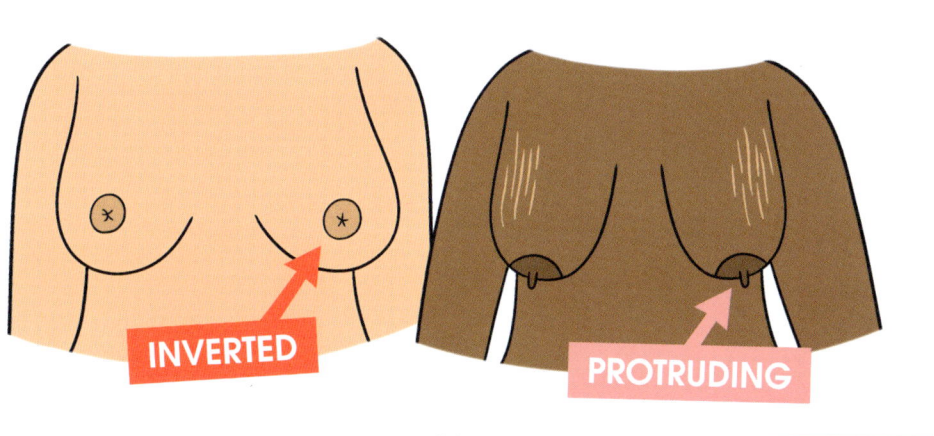

INVERTED

PROTRUDING

FLAT

PUFFY

BUMPY

HAIRY

ONE INVERTED

EXTRA NIPPLE

Itchy nipples (and boobs)!

The nipples, areolae and skin of the boob can itch when the skin is being stretched during boob growth. Some people find a firm garment like a crop top made of soft, breathable fabric like cotton, hemp or bamboo helps relieve the itch. But itching during this time is really common!

> In summer, when it gets sweaty, or if I've had food I'm a bit allergic to, my nipples get itchy. There's no rash, they don't look sore or red, but that's where the itch decides to plant itself. *Berno*

> At random times, like walking, there'll be a random itch and I'll be like (to my boob), 'You didn't have to do that'! *Amy, 13*

> I think it's generally when I get sweaty that it gets really itchy, all over! Certain times it's itchier. I try not to scratch in public. I'll subtly adjust my bra and itch it at the same time! *Olive, 14*

People who have eczema or psoriasis (common skin conditions) might have flare-ups during puberty that may or may not affect the nipple, causing a rash or itch. Flare-ups can occur during the rest of your life, particularly if your skin reacts to allergens. Remember that your boobs are like any other part of your body – they benefit from an airing-out once in a while!

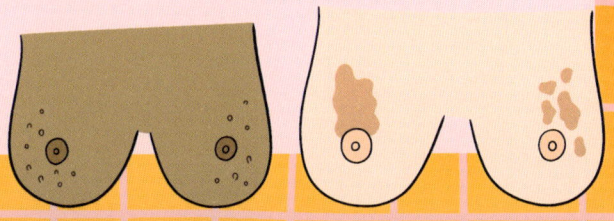

MORE COMMON BOOB WORRIES

Worries about boobs are super common, but real-life problems with boobs are not. So don't be tempted to stress out! Read this book thoroughly.

MORE ON p. 141

There should be an answer within, and you can always see a doctor if you are really worried.

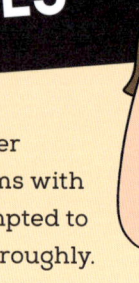

Sore, hurty boobs

Whether your boobs grow to be small, big or in-between, there's a **lot** going on as they develop during puberty. There is a potential breastmilk factory being constructed! New types of cells are growing and forming 'units' that can make milk, held together by tough support tissues. All this action means soreness during this time can be natural 'growing pain' and it can happen early in Stages Two to Four.

MORE ON p. 63

MORE ON p. 12

When your periods start, your boobs have usually done most of their developing and a lot of those growing pains will have settled down. A person's very first period usually happens around Stage Four of boob development. However, it takes a year or two for the period hormones to get into their own 'cycle' – the menstrual cycle. Once this happens, these period hormones can cause boobs to swell and subside at different times of your cycle in a way that can be predicted. So it's likely to be a few years after the start of your boob development that you experience regular period-related boob changes. The menstrual cycle can cause boob discomfort for some people in the week leading up to your period.

Wearing a firm garment such as a crop top or firm-fitting bra can help relieve sore, hurty puberty boobs, although it depends on the individual. Other people find anything too firm against their boobs makes it worse.

QUESTIONS FOR DR MELISSA

Lumpy boobs

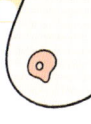

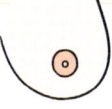

> **I have a lump on my boob underneath my nipple. I haven't told anyone because it is too embarrassing! What could it be? What should I do?**

Breast tissue, which appears at the earliest stage of puberty underneath the nipple, feels different to anything else in your body. It takes a while to get to know. The very first sign of breast development is the 'breast bud' and it can sometimes feel like a single lump underneath the nipple.

As puberty boobs grow, there will be some that feel lumpier than others. It's to do with the proportions of breast, support and fat tissues in boobs, which varies between people and is completely normal. Breast cancer is extremely uncommon in teenagers.

MORE ON p. 12

MORE ON p. 63

A NOTE FROM THE DOCTOR (MELISSA)

Boys with boobs

Boys would sometimes write to the magazine column Dolly Doctor asking me why they had boobs. Some were completely panicked and thought it meant puberty had gone horribly wrong for them. When I've seen boys who have puberty boobs in my clinic, they don't bring the topic up spontaneously. They're often wearing baggy clothes and I might only notice because I'm listening to their chest with my stethoscope and lifting up their shirt. So I then mention puberty boobs to them and have found it brings huge relief to be able to talk about it. When I explain that for the great majority of boys, puberty boobs go away completely, it might be partly reassuring. But I know it doesn't always change the way they feel about going into changing rooms at school or about what other kids might say or think. Part of this has to do with how we think about females and males and their bodies.

MORE ON p. 100

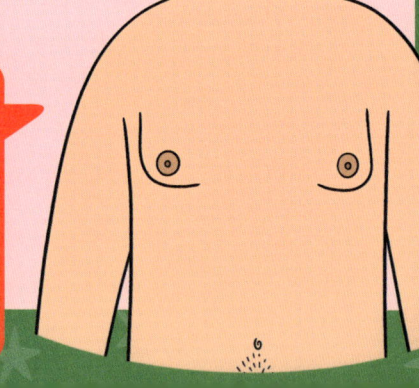

> That's how I definitely noticed them first. I remember thinking, 'Am I putting on weight?' and I started seeing them in photos. I was solid but not fat. They would come out enough to cause a little bit of a stretch on the shirt, kind of thing. *JB*

> I distinctly remember getting changed for a swimming carnival in Year Ten or so, and a couple of older guys started to point and laugh but I'd developed a strategy to make them go down (if you squeezed the nipple they would go down). I was also part of a progressive peer group, so I was never bullied. Fortunately! *Andrew*

> Swimming classes with school were horrible. I'd wear a T-shirt in the pool thinking that'd help and it just made it worse. Growing up in the 1970s and 1980s, there was no filter on body-shaming. *Dan*

Over fifty per cent of boys going through puberty will develop puberty boobs. They are usually smallish and not noticeable when the boy's wearing clothes. They look like a bit of swelling under the nipple. The nipples and areolae don't enlarge as much as girls' do. Sometimes they grow larger and look like a small, round breast. Puberty boobs in boys mostly go away after six months to two years, although the underlying breast tissue remains. All humans have breast tissue, which is why anyone can get breast cancer, including men.

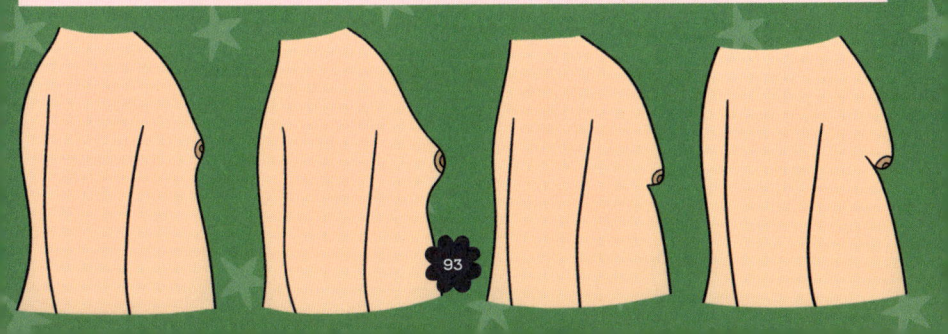

MORE ON p. 10

JB'S EXPERIENCE

I'D BEEN PREPARED FOR THE SURPRISING ERECTIONS, THE VOICE CHANGE, ALL OF THAT, BUT I HADN'T BEEN PREPARED FOR THIS.

I started to get 'breasts' before I started to get the other stages of puberty. They looked like what an overweight man would have. I reckon I was about thirteen when they started to come on. (This is the first conversation I've had about it my whole life, and I've been married for ten years!)

I was solid but not fat.

I was horrified. Absolutely horrified.

I was in an amazing family but not one where anyone would talk about it. I remember being given the puberty books, but that was it – I had to figure out the boobs thing by myself.

No-one else noticed, and the only time I remember someone bringing it up was when we got new school uniforms and a guy who did weights came up to me and said, "Wow, you've been working out, your chest is huge!" Knowing exactly what he was talking about, I said, "Yeah, man, just taking care of myself," implying that I'd been working out. It can give that appearance of muscle or some sort of mass there under clothes.

I remember being really self-conscious. In showers, at the swimming pool.

I had to go into a wheelchair when I was seventeen. Suddenly that became the defining physical feature. The man boobs become less noticeable when you're in the chair, then you build your upper body strength, then by the time I was out of my chair aged twenty two, they were sort of gone.

So many things I've got through in my life with the knowledge that they're temporary. But denying something gives it SO MUCH oxygen. Joking or talking about the boobs thing would've given me some normalcy. You know, if my dad had said, 'I went through it, you're going through it – you're going to be fine.' As a fifteen-year-old that would've meant a lot.

I feel shy about my boobs!

Pretty much everyone we spoke to when we were writing this book went through a phase of extreme self-consciousness about their bodies, and particularly their boobs. It usually hit when they were around eleven or twelve and went until they were about fourteen, and it can be described as **always worrying about how you look, wanting to cover up** and **feeling exposed and embarrassed.**

Over the twenty-plus years that I wrote for the magazine column Dolly Doctor, (where teens sent in anonymous questions) there were so many questions about boobs. Although some related to discomfort or lumps, the majority were about appearance. There was a lot of worry that boobs looked weird or different from everyone else.

I think the fact that many teens still feel this way (and the fact that I once did too, as did my mother and my grandmother) speaks to the self-consciousness of adolescence. And also the pressure that girls feel to look a certain way.

We might not be able to do much about adolescent self-consciousness – except to explain that it will pass, and everything will feel OK. But we can and should keep trying to do something about the pressure that many people – and especially girls and women – feel about their appearance.

Dr Melissa

Experiencing shyness, worry, and obsessive thinking about your boobs is **SO** common! It's a private thing that you go through on your own personal timetable, and you have no control over it. You don't necessarily get to share it with your friends because everyone's on a different track. And not only do you have to learn a bunch of 'management' techniques to deal with your new boobs – like bras and sturdy swimwear – you might also have to deal with your boobs suddenly attracting unwanted attention.

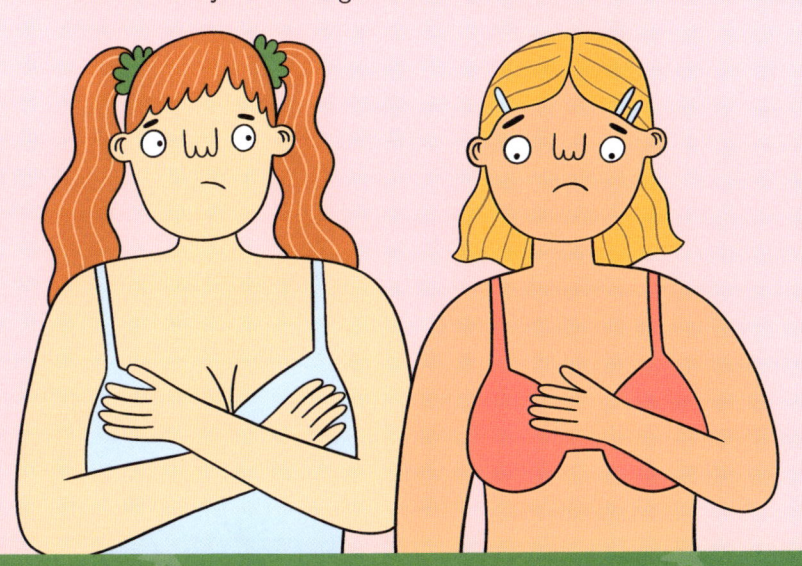

> Whenever I'm wearing, like, a smaller top or something I feel like people are staring at me from all around, and I'm putting my arms over my chest – crossing my arms defensively. *Amy, 13*

I'm worried that people are looking at me, and it makes me uncomfortable. I always thought I looked flat and undeveloped – especially in school uniform. *Rosie, 13*

I feel like I need to prepare myself for swimming ... shaving, double-checking nothing's fallen out. My body checks get a lot higher when I'm swimming. I don't want to swim in front of certain people – in front of most people! *Dee Dee, 16*

All this coincides with a whole lot of puberty changes that really cause havoc on your moods, emotions and relationships – as well as your body!

The good news? It will pass. With practice, you'll care less about being looked at (and maybe it doesn't happen as often as you think). And you'll get used to choosing garments that make you feel good and are comfortable to wear.

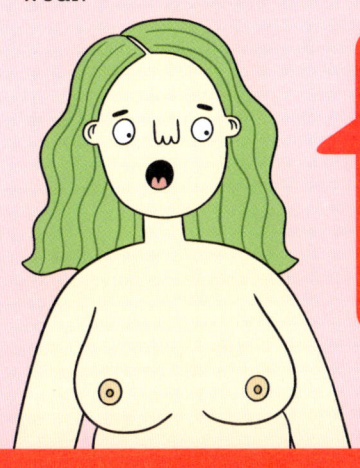

> I used to worry about what people thought of me, but I just got kind of YOLO about everything. It's kind of just like, people are gonna judge you, but you just care less. I mean, I care a LOT about my friends' opinions but less about others'. *Gracie N. 14*

> For the first time, there's the thought – 'I look good and now I'm going to let go of this constant nagging that's going on in the back of my head.' Growing up has been about choosing to have a better, more carefree time if I just let go of this worry and this anxiety about how I look. Which doesn't just happen in one go! *Lily. 17*

A NOTE ABOUT BOOBS, GENDER AND GENDER IDENTITY

Gender is a word that describes the way we think about being female, male, neither, both or something else. These ideas come from the society around us. A simple example might be that in today's world, pink is seen as a 'girl's colour'. But there were times when pink was considered a boy's colour. There's no biological rule nor reason why certain colours belong to a particular gender – we make these up, and certain beliefs stick for a while. Some people are born with female or male genitals but, as they grow and look at the world around them, they do not see themselves as belonging to that gender. The way we see ourselves in relation to gender is called gender identity.

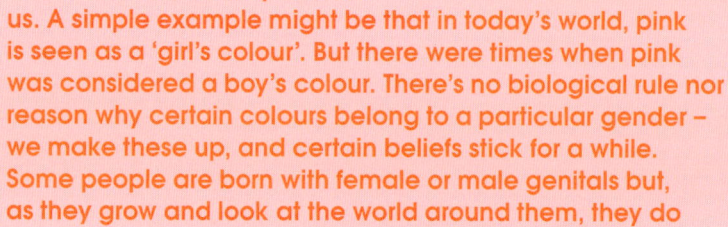

Gender identity is deeply personal and describes your deeply held feelings about whether you're male, female, both, neither. It's different from the sex that was recorded when you were born.

Our interpretation of someone's gender is influenced by the culture we live in. For example: hair. It's common in many cultures for people to follow gender 'rules'

about hair – that **girls** have long hair and **boys** have short hair. People who break the rules often encounter surprise and even aggression – even from those who understand and agree that there's no **reason** why boys can't have long hair and girls short! So the way that hair is 'gendered' is because of society and culture, not because of, like, biology or some sort of basic human survival need.

Another good example: as we've learned, lots of boys develop puberty breasts for a few years. Some of the men we spoke to still have theirs. That doesn't make them any less 'male'. They are still exactly who they always were. But, just as hair is a 'signifier' that a person is a certain gender, breasts signify someone is female. So developing breasts can be confronting for a boy – especially one who feels insecure about his 'maleness' or masculinity. Hostility, judgement and shame around boys' breasts is unhelpful and actually really uncool: why is it that something perceived as 'female' can be seen as inherently bad if adopted by a male? Are women so inferior? Of course not!

For a lot of young women and girls, the appearance of breasts can make them feel 'feminine' or 'womanly', or it can be something that has no real influence on their experience of their gender. Developing boobs can be unpleasant if the girl getting them doesn't feel quite ready to be a 'woman' or doesn't want to be sexualized. And not developing breasts can be confronting for a girl who is anxiously waiting for them. Many people want and expect breasts to grow but still take a while to feel entirely at ease about them.

It's a different story altogether if having boobs (or not having them) profoundly affects your gender identity. Developing or not developing boobs can be particularly difficult for trans and gender-diverse kids and adolescents

MORE ON p. 191

because they feel a total mismatch between their bodies and their gender identities. When puberty hits and boobs grow on a trans boy (who identifies as male), it might be distressing for them because boobs are associated with female bodies and identities. A trans girl (who identifies as female) might want to grow boobs because it would affirm their identity as female. Gender-diverse or non-binary people might not identify as either 'female' or 'male'. How they feel about boobs growing or not growing depends on ... well, just them and nothing else.

SUE FIGHTS LIKE A GIRL!

IS THERE SOMETHING WRONG WITH THAT?

NO ...

THEN DON'T SAY IT LIKE IT'S AN INSULT!

IF OTHER PEOPLE'S GENDER IS CONFUSING TO YOU, REMEMBER SOMETHING ACTIVIST HAYDEN MOON SAYS: 'TRANS PEOPLE ARE THEIR GENDER, THE END.' GENDER IS NOT A RIDDLE FOR YOU TO SOLVE – IT'S AN IDENTITY FOR YOU TO ACCEPT.

Being transgender is defined as feeling 'a marked and persistent incongruence between a person's experienced gender and their assigned sex'. In other words? A person's experienced gender does not fit in well with their assigned sex. So maybe when they were born, everyone like the doctors and their parents agreed that they were a boy, but they themselves never felt like a boy.

The World Health Organization now accepts that being transgender is not a mental health condition. Gender incongruence is not pathological. It is part of the regular, everyday spectrum of human existence.

BOOBS ARE MORE THAN JUST BODY PARTS

Why do boobs get so much attention?

Breasts symbolise the start of adulthood and sexual desirability in a lot of cultures. This has made them both taboo and appealing – a heady combination! But liking boobs is not always about sexiness – even innocent babies find breasts appealing.

The truth is, boobs are wonderful. They are a beautiful part of the human body. To many people, across race and culture, boobs are attractive. Breasts have an inherent appeal to everyone from newborns to teenagers to the middle-aged and ancient, from straight girls to gay guys!

Boobs attract attention. They can mean something to cuddle, something to caress, or just a way to fill a bra, bikini or T-shirt. They can mean breastfeeding, softness, sexiness. They can mean the perfect curve, a pleasing line. Boobs also change over time, which adds to their mystery! They might draw attention because you once didn't have them – and suddenly, now you do.

Breasts are endlessly interesting because, generally, there's a sameness to most people – we all get a head and a heart and most of us have two hands and two legs. But boobs can be all different shapes and sizes, and that inspires a curiosity about them.

Body image and boobs

Boobs can have a big effect on our body image, especially when they're developing and growing. They can take some serious getting used to! Our boobs can influence how **attractive** we feel, how 'male' or 'female' we feel, how grown-up we feel, and whether we think we're desirable. And that's a pretty heavy burden for a pair of body parts to carry, don't you think?!

In an ideal world, we'd all love everything about our bodies, all the time! But in real life, many of us have days when we love our body mixed in with a few times when we think we should look more like some of the celebrities we see in the media.

There's an important difference between a healthy body image – mostly feeling relaxed and accepting of how you look, and treating your body well – and an unhealthy body image, where **all** you can see are the 'negatives' and 'flaws' and things you want to change. Negative body image is a major bummer because it tricks you into thinking that your LOOKS DETERMINE YOUR WORTH as a person – and they DON'T!

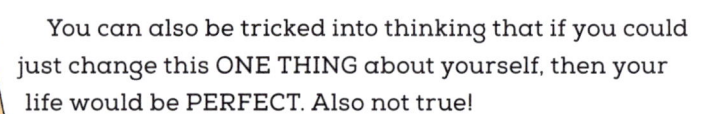

You can also be tricked into thinking that if you could just change this ONE THING about yourself, then your life would be PERFECT. Also not true!

An old guy called Teddy Roosevelt once said, **'Comparison is the thief of joy.'** It's SUCH a good line.

If you find yourself comparing your body with others', particularly those of people whose JOB it is to be 'professionally gorgeous', you will almost certainly feel less-than, or crummy, or worthless. You let the joy thief in!

Models and the 'professionally gorgeous' (who are only 'gorgeous' according to society's ideals, which change with time and fashion) usually start with great genes, and then add a gruelling, daily pursuit of 'gorgeousness' – from dieting and surgery to beauty appointments, workouts, spray tans, teeth whitening and hair treatments. It's almost certainly not achievable for most people, and anyway – surely you have more badass things to be doing with your time?

Boobs and sexualization

What is 'sexualization'?

Sexualization is seeing someone or something in sexual terms. It's done without any buy-in or consent from the person or thing in question. For example, 'the patient was constantly sexualising the nurses'. The patient sees the nurses as sexy, and communicates that – even though the nurses don't want it, ask for it or agree to it.

When a young person starts growing breasts, it can be a real shock to discover that their breasts attract unwanted sexualisation from others. Most of us are so young when our breasts start to develop that we're really not ready to deal with being sexualized! It can be gross and upsetting. It can add to our self-consciousness. And it can make us feel vulnerable and scared.

Getting boobs can mean people suddenly start treating us as if we're older than our real age.

WHEN IT'S A STRANGER, IT CAN MANIFEST AS STREET HARASSMENT:

SEXUALZATION CAN BE WHEN SOMEONE IS:

- Assuming you're up for romantic or sexual attention based on how you look.
- Staring at your breasts or other body parts.
- Looking only at your breasts.
- Making sexually explicit or other derogatory comments.
- Saying things like, 'You look older.'

- Following you or blocking your path.
- Filming you.
- Flashing their genitals at you.
- Making whistling noises or kissing noises at you.
- Leering at you or making suggestive gestures at you.
- Barking or making other noises at you.
- Calling out, "Give us a smile!" or other maddening instructions.

STREET HARASSMENT 101

1. You're <u>not</u> imagining it.
2. How people treat you is not your fault.
3. If you hate it, that's valid.

Do I have to live with being sexualized?

No. You can call it out, video it, engage bystanders, walk away, call the police, demand they stop or all of the above. Studies have shown that people who react in the moment to street harassment usually feel better afterwards, compared with those who kept quiet. *(This doesn't mean you have to, though!)* Creepy or insulting behaviours can escalate into dangerous behaviours. You should do what feels right for you in the moment; trust your instincts. It's OK to get away from the situation. It doesn't have to be a big scene, it can just be, 'Hmmm, see ya, bye.'

To avoid being sexualized, some people wear clothes that obscure their shape. (For instance, Yumi favours a denim jacket, stiff cotton shirts, or a hoodie and T-shirt combination, oversized tees, etc, and avoids clothes that show lots of skin, tummy or cleavage.) As you get older, sexualisation does become less embarrassing – not because it happens less, but perhaps you grow desensitized to it. Most of us learn to dress, carry ourselves and defend ourselves against sexualization and street harassment. Some people can deal with it at a high level, others can't stand it at all. Again, that doesn't make it OK or 'normal'. It's gross.

What if I WANT to dress sexy?

You have every right to dress sexy! Dressing sexy can be totally fun and is a rite of passage for many teenagers. Wearing clothes that show off cleavage doesn't make it OK for others to harass you.

When you're on the receiving end of unwanted sexualization, you don't owe it to anyone to be 'nice'. Do what you have to do to feel safe, and do it on your terms – whether that's sticking with friends in a group, making sure your phone is fully charged, taking pictures of harassers on your phone, or telling creeps to get lost.

What should I do?

Women and girls are conditioned to be 'quiet' and 'nice'. It can be quite powerful to be loud and unpleasant! Imagine you're in a shopping centre and someone is harassing you. If you shout, in your biggest voice, **"GET AWAY FROM ME, YOU'RE SCARING ME, I DON'T KNOW YOU!"** then no-one will think you've done something wrong, and all eyes will turn to the perpetrator.

DON'T BE AFRAID TO BE LOUD. IT'S POWERFUL!

What can I say/yell?

- Ugh, gross!
- Please go away and don't talk to me.
- That is a creepy thing to say.
- I'm twelve. Why would you say that?
- WHY ARE YOU STARING, ARE YOU OK?
- Women really don't like that.
- Do you realize that you're making me feel really uncomfortable?

Not everyone wants boobs

When I originally started getting boobs, my friends were like, "YAY, we're getting boobs now, we're women! WHOOOO!" But for me – I didn't like getting boobs. I was sporty, and when you have boobs it opens up to other people or guys in your year group commenting on them, or you're presenting yourself as more feminine, or more grown-up, and I didn't really like that because I was a big tomboy and didn't like to stand out. *Yash, 16*

While getting boobs can be an exciting indication that you're growing up, there are a lot of people who are NOT excited. It can be an inconvenience. It can be something you're just not into. This doesn't make you weird – it's actually pretty common.

I was worried about being teased. I noticed the boys at school looking more and that made me really self-conscious, so I remember going up a size in my school uniform and just wanting everything I wore to be tent-like, and just wanting the silhouette to reveal nothing. I ended up wearing black T-shirts all the time. *Berno*

The best thing to do is experiment – with binding, with different shirts – shirts with colourful prints and designs is the best way to disguise your chest if that's what you're feeling uncomfortable about. *Skylar, 23*

MORE ON p. 192

I don't want to get boobs at all! Cos I don't want to wear a bra. Because it seems really itchy and I don't like how they look. *Florence, 8*

Sexism and boobs

Sexism means discrimination against someone because of their sex or gender. It happens much more to girls and women than to boys and men. One of the ways sexism is expressed is the fact that girls' bodies are criticised, commented on, and given attention way more than boys' bodies are. For instance, a girl might feel pressured to have a narrow waist while a boy could go his whole adolescence without ever thinking about his own waist!

Language changes all the time, so it's tricky to get specific about any particular word for 'boob' being wrong or right. But you know how there are some words for 'breast' that seem demeaning, or unnecessarily sexual, or imply that just having breasts is inherently bad? Well, guess what: those words are sexist and offensive. Put them in the bin!

(And by the way, a **word** being offensive doesn't mean the **thing** itself is offensive. It just means that there are more formal or 'professional' ways of naming them.)

I dislike the word 'hooters' as it implies catcalling, like, 'People were hooting out their car windows as they drove by.' And I really hate 'knockers' because breasts don't 'knock' together, nor do they make a 'knocking' sound – it's an ugly use of language. And I detest 'honkers' because the image I get is a stranger thinking they can 'honk' on the end of your breast like it's a comedy horn. *Yumi*

Appearance

There's also a lot of sexism in the attention given to a girl's appearance: the clothes she wears, her hair and make-up can all be the subject of other people's focus, instead of the girl herself. It's annoying because it's both boring and unfair, and it can waste a girl's time and energy when she'd rather be focusing on something important, like working on a cure for cancer or making her friends laugh or climate-change activism.

Boys and men are much less likely to be scrutinised in the same way. Nor are they expected to LISTEN to criticisms about their appearance. If you've ever noticed a news article that comments on the way a woman in politics dresses – but never once mentions her male colleagues' suits – you'll know exactly what we're talking about!

> I once gave a speech that I thought was pretty good and afterwards the feedback I got was, 'You shouldn't wear yellow, it makes your skin look washed out'. *Yumi*

ALSO COMMON IS PEOPLE MAKING ASSUMPTIONS ABOUT SOMEONE'S SEXUAL THOUGHTS, ATTITUDES OR EXPERIENCE BECAUSE OF THEIR BOOBS.

> I can be in a tight top and it's like, 'Roar, she's up for it!' And my friend who's a B-cup can be in exactly the same kind of outfit and she's not considered up for it. *Berno*

NEVER ASKING FOR IT

Boobs can be the subject of incredibly sexist attitudes. The sexism might be obvious, e.g. derogatory comments or humiliating compliments being made about a person's boobs, as if breasts are the only things that matter about a person. Or it can be subtle and insidious, like someone staring at your chest. Either way, it is NOT OK.

Catcalling

A catcall is when someone you don't know shouts something out on the street – it can be something like, 'Hey, baby!', 'Give us a smile!' Or, 'Nice tits.' Or a noise, like wooting, barking or whistling.

Comments, stares and catcalls can make you feel objectified and unsafe. Sometimes it's subtle and non-verbal, like a look that makes you feel like your body is something shameful. It would be difficult for you to report it or complain about it because it's often done so that only you notice, or it doesn't feel like a big enough deal to draw attention to – even though it can have a severe impact on your mood.

It might be a stranger whistling at you, or a leering look. It might be something verbal, like a question or comment that is seemingly neutral: "Why are you wearing that?" or "That's a nice top." Or, "How old are you?" Make no mistake – these kinds of behaviours are about power. The people **objectifying** you are trying to exert power over you and make you feel small. They are making your appearance the central focus and dehumanizing you.

I got some comments when I was younger – as a young adult, I had men in the street say to me, "Lovely face, shame about the chest." Complete strangers! Commenting because I'm so flat! I was so shocked that I didn't react. *Laura*

There have been a few times in public that I've worn tops that are a little deeper cut than what I would normally wear and men who are ten years older than me stare me down, which is totally gross. It wasn't so much me being self-conscious about my body and more about being conscious about my safety. *Cleo, 15*

There are different ways you can choose to react, depending on the situation. Calling it out, staring it down, making a rude gesture or telling the person to get lost – these are all options, but safety is key.

In some situations I have very clearly told men to f**k off. But for the most part I don't even look at them. They are invisible to me. I am a queen and queens walk past this scum. *Yumi*

Boys comment about girls' boobs, I don't know if they do that more when I'm not around but I've definitely heard them say stuff. Usually the girls stick up for the other girls. *Gracie N. 14*

Compliments

A 'compliment' can mask sexism – for example, telling someone they have nice boobs could be completely inappropriate, embarrassing and deeply humiliating, even though it's a 'compliment' – depending on the context.

> **Your boobs are bigger, right?**

Sometimes male friends have said to me, "Have you had a boob job?" and it's really none of their business. I think that it's really not appropriate in a social situation to make remarks about people's bodies like that. *Catharine Lumby*

Imagine telling someone they have ugly boobs, fat boobs, or that their boobs are too small or too big or too anything. It's never cool, and it's always inappropriate. So too are compliments. A compliment draws attention to a part of you – whether it's 'You are the bravest person here,' or 'You're our strongest goal shooter,' or 'You have great eyes.' Unless you have the type of intimate friendship or romantic relationship where compliments about your boobs are mutually accepted, anyone giving compliments about your boobs is crossing a line and probably knows it.

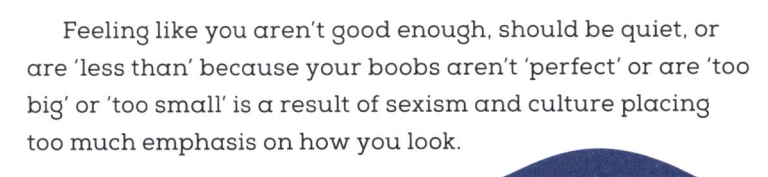

Feeling like you aren't good enough, should be quiet, or are 'less than' because your boobs aren't 'perfect' or are 'too big' or 'too small' is a result of sexism and culture placing too much emphasis on how you look.

MOST OF US **GROW OUT OF OBSESSING ABOUT HOW WE LOOK, BUT CARING ABOUT OUR APPEARANCE IS A BIT OF A FIXTURE OF TEENAGEHOOD. THERE IS A HACK, THOUGH! ACCEPTING THAT YOU'RE PERFECTLY OK JUST AS YOU ARE GETS EASIER – ONCE YOU START ACCEPTING OTHERS JUST AS THEY ARE.**

You are enough!

Sexism and nipples

There's a lot of sexism when it comes to the appearance of boobs, and you'll likely notice it in the appearance of nipples in media. Some social media platforms censor pictures that contain female nipples – but not male ones. This throws up all kinds of dilemmas for users. Some people have made fun of this rule by photoshopping out their 'female' nipples and replacing them with 'male' nipples. The photos look exactly the same! It's hilarious, and it shines a light on how meaningless these rules are. A movement called #freethenipple aims to expose the sexism of these rules.

On TV and in films, you'll notice that a character rarely has erect nipples in a scene unless it's to draw attention to her sexuality. But in reality, the cold makes nipples hard ALL THE TIME and has nothing to do with feeling horny. It's the weather!

> I deliberately dress so that my nipples never show. At home I'm not so worried about it but in public I keep an eye on it. *Yash, 16*

In the clothes you buy and the bras that are available, there are a lot of layers of 'protection' in place to hide a girl's erect nipples from the world. This is all fine if that's what the wearer WANTS – if she doesn't want her nipples to be seen. But working off the assumption that a girl SHOULDN'T allow her nipples to stick through her clothes is really asking her to fight biology for no other reason than that it's what OTHER people want.

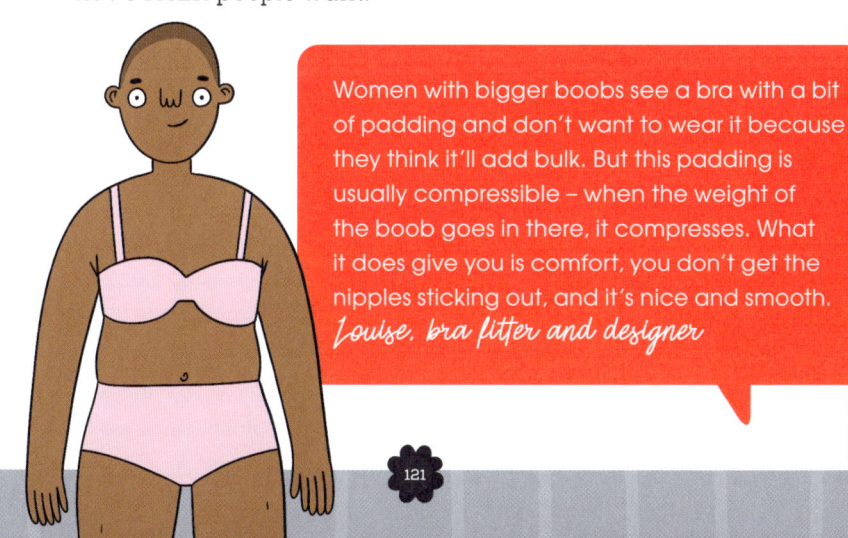

> Women with bigger boobs see a bra with a bit of padding and don't want to wear it because they think it'll add bulk. But this padding is usually compressible – when the weight of the boob goes in there, it compresses. What it does give you is comfort, you don't get the nipples sticking out, and it's nice and smooth.
> *Louise, bra fitter and designer*

> There was a girl at my school who developed early and was often talked about because you could see her nipples, and it was a big message to me that if you can see your nipples through your shirt, it's inappropriate. My opinion has changed – when I see women in hippy communities walking around with no bra it's not a sexual thing, it's just a comfort thing. *Dee Dee, 16*

Transphobia and sexism

Discrimination and harassment on the basis of gender identity is called **transphobia**. It happens for a number of reasons, including ignorance and fear of people who don't fit a certain stereotype. Discrimination and harassment might take the form of making derogatory comments and using offensive words or nicknames, putting someone down, deliberately getting their pronouns wrong (saying 'he' when they have asked to be 'she', for example), bullying (online or in person) or ignoring someone or leaving them out. It can also involve physical aggression and violence. Discrimination and harassment on the basis of someone's gender identity, race or cultural background is not only wrong, it can be a crime. Being the victim of transphobic discrimination and harassment is one reason why trans and gender-diverse people experience poor mental health compared to others.

For some trans and gender-diverse people, transphobia AND sexism lead to 'double discrimination'. This is where two forms of discrimination intersect with each other,

MORE ON p. 191

having an even bigger negative impact. A trans girl might be taunted, harassed or discriminated against for being trans but also for being female: her body is up for scrutiny just as it is for cisgender girls and women (cisgender means you identify as the gender you were assigned at birth). A trans boy might experience discrimination for being trans and for not conforming to a 'male stereotype'.

So what does all this have to do with boobs and growing up, and what should we do about it? Here's a simple answer: when puberty starts, we suddenly become very conscious of our body and what's happening to it. We begin to associate these changes with other things such as attractiveness, function, sex and gender identity. And people who are afraid of things they don't understand, or who need to make themselves feel good by putting down others, can say or do things that diminish, disrespect or discriminate. This sort of body-related intimidation or harassment is more likely to happen to you if you're a woman, or trans or non-binary person. And it's worse again if you're a person of colour. It's never OK. So call it out, report it, and never, ever do it yourself.
Please.
Thank you.

Boobs and race

Race and culture play a big part in how we think about our own boobs. Culture is all about what's common where you live, in your family, at school and in what you see around you – on your phone, in books, TV and stuff. But race can have a big influence as well, and it doesn't matter where you live.

I'm Blasian – a mix of Black and Asian – and my boobs are a mix of Malaysian and Xhosa. Massive, nut brown areolae. My mum has great boobs – beautiful, mango-shaped – and I loved my boobs from the moment they formed. My sisters hated their boobs and I think it was because they were always looking at them in relation to white women's boobs. *Candy*

Most Chinese women are pretty flat-chested so I can't say there was a lot of expectation about getting boobs when I was growing up – other than that (according to my family) I was supposed to feed LOTS OF BABIES with them! So … happy days when I found out there were so many other fun things I could do with them! What used to worry me was that my nipples were never going to be pink like all those Harlequin heroines. I'm over it now – dark brown and proud! *Miranda*

I didn't really have an expectation about how they would look because Greek women come in all shapes and sizes. I can tell you that the outlook was pretty conservative – topless sunbathing was definitely frowned upon and there was an expectation to keep covered up. *Alexandra*

Growing up with foster parents, one Australian, one British, nothing was ever really talked about. It was all very hushed tones, so I didn't know what to expect. I got my period – the next day there were pads on my bed. I got to high school and suddenly had to start wearing bras. *Elaine*

Japanese women aren't known for their hefty bosoms so I never expected to have much boobage! *Yumi*

Filipinos are so ethnically mixed – boob size varied! My mum and grandma used to tell me that the curves and brown skin came from the Spanish side and the boobless slim shape with pale skin came from the Chinese side. No scientific proof, of course! It's likely the women in my family racially profiled cup size back in the day! *Mary*

My Latina mum was quite hourglass-shaped and had decent C cups. I kind of knew (but mostly hoped) that's what I'd end up looking like! At the same time Kate Moss's tiny bumps were the fashion and to this day I cannot show their shape in clothing without feeling exposed. *Marihuzka*

POOJA'S EXPERIENCE

I grew up in Australia but my parents migrated from India and were quite conservative Hindus. In my culture, girls who came of age were told to cover up by the family matriarchs and to date I don't recall a single conversation being had about boobs.

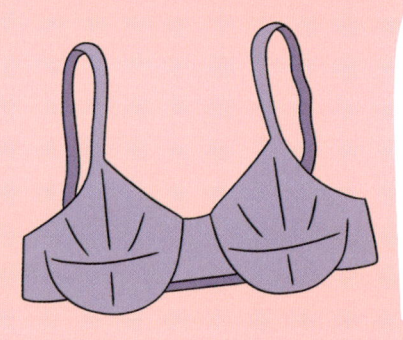

> THE MESSAGE WAS THAT BREASTS WERE A SIGN OF SEXUALITY AND MUST NEVER BE PUT ON DISPLAY, NOT EVEN FOR BREASTFEEDING.

If you had them on display (even by accident) you'd receive some stern words from your aunties or mum about 'what will people say'. I was expected never to put my family in such a position of shame and judgement.

I was a shy teen so really onboarded my cultural shame and tried to cover myself up and draw as little attention to myself as possible, especially considering I was an overweight kid. Luckily, my all-girls school was racially diverse and there was no name-calling there, but I definitely had larger breasts than most girls at my school. Going bra shopping was mortifying as breasts my size at that age were relegated to the boring bra section instead of the cute padded ones everyone else chose. I remember my long hair (another Indian tradition) getting caught underneath them in my sleep, and to this day underwire bras give me a rash.

When I got into my late teens and early twenties I kept hearing my mother's inner dialogue about breasts and sexuality and modesty, but that was also the time I started to gain a lot more independence and became more empowered about my body, breasts and the sexuality that comes along with them.

I GREW UP IN THE 1990s, WHEN SMALL BREASTS AND WAIFISHLY THIN FRAMES WERE IN (THINK KATE MOSS).

Now our poster women for female sexiness are bodies like Kim Kardashian's, with big boobs and big butts. The tables have really turned on what it means to be sexy!

BOOB CHALLENGES

Living with my dad

If you live with your dad and you are starting to get boobs, you may find it tricky to talk to him about what's ahead. Will he take you bra shopping? Does he know why your nipples are itching? What cup size does he think you'll grow to? What clothes can you wear to feel most comfortable?

Some dads are awesome at these conversations. Others may try, but don't know the answers. And there will be some dads who get embarrassed and clam right up! None of these make your dad right or wrong – he's just being who he is.

> My dad and I are pretty close – he was the first person I told when I got my period. He came with me to the shops but he kind of hung around in the men's section and I just picked out my bra and then he paid. *Olive, 14*

My dad was a single dad; there was not a female here to have this conversation with. What struck me afterwards was that he wanted to have the conversation with me because he didn't know if I needed it, if it was necessary, or if I was having these conversations with someone else. It's important to remember that your parents want to help you out – they're not WANTING it to be awkward! They don't want to make you suffer. Naturally, they want to give you a hand with something that is going to help out your day-to-day life. *Lily, 17*

There are a couple of ways to deal with all this, and there's a chance your dad may have already set one of these ideas in motion:

Option 1: Drag Dad along

Do some research and then enlist your dad as your helper, bank and cheer squad. Your research will hopefully give you some ballpark figures of what you're in for – for instance, how much money you'll probably be spending on your first two bras. Dad can drive you to the shops and hang out while you try bras on. He can pay for your stuff when the time comes.

FOREWARN YOUR DAD SO HE KNOWS WHAT HE'S IN FOR.

Option 2: Outsource to aunty

An 'aunty' figure might be an older female friend, your dad's sister, partner or bestie, gay uncle, grandma, nanny, babysitter, etc. This person might be called upon to take you shopping for bras and help out in any other situations where your dad's lack of lived experience requires outside input. They may be someone you can call on the phone when you have a quick question that doesn't warrant a full sit-down or outing. It's OK to make this set-up semi-official by saying, "Can I call you if I have any boob questions?" or something like that.

- AUNTY
- BROTHER'S GF
- BFF'S STEP MUM
- SISTER
- SISTER'S GF
- BABYSITTER
- GRANDMA

My nonna taught me to hide all kinds of stuff in my bra. She always used to have, like, a fifty pound note, or a ciggie, or even a gold coin in her bra. I think one night I literally put a couple of French fries in my bra in case I wanted them later! *Berno*

Option 3: Be an independent kid

There's a whole spectrum of hands-on parenting – and lack thereof! – that kids survive. Sometimes a young person does a whole lot more independent caring for themselves than others do. This might mean shopping by yourself for bras. If it feels better, take a friend along for a second opinion ('Do these straps dig in too much at the back?') and really work on getting the advice of a professional bra fitter who works at a store.

I bought my first bra from the lingerie basket in the middle of this charity shop and then just wore it all the time. I thought, 'Oh, well! I'm gonna have to do this myself, I guess!' *Clem. 39*

I'm good

Hanging out the washing

If you live in a situation where it's just you and your dad, or two dads, or an all-male household, or even just a household where your dad does most of the washing, then there may be confusion or awkwardness around handling your bras. We have heard of some dads feeling a bit shy about hanging their daughters' bras out to dry – a combo of not wanting to cross a line and not wanting to do it wrong!

If this is your situation, you don't have to make a big deal about it. You could say, "Hey, I'm going to handle all the washing of my bras, OK?" Or, "Dad, these items are handwash only, so if you come across them, just leave them in the laundry bucket, please!"

If your dad, brother, stepsibling or main male carer does all the washing, maybe point out the section in this book on bra care and make sure they read it so they know how to do it right. Perhaps you can have a conversation about how you'd best like it done.

MORE ON p. 52

The clanger comment

Sometimes a person makes a comment about your body that really stays with you. They may not have said it to be mean or nasty, but it sticks in your mind and can have devastating consequences.

It's a common story from so many people. Maybe if they were older (or younger!), the comment would have made them shrug, or say, "Meh," or they wouldn't have registered it. But because they heard it at a tender time, during a vulnerable stage in development, it really landed and felt very hurtful.

> No matter what kind of breasts you have, you will find that men and boys will comment on them. It's just rude. *Catharine Lumby*

> My dad made a comment when my boobs started growing. He said, "Oh, they're like little acorns." And I remember thinking, "OH MY GOD," and being really, really mortified. I think as a male you just shouldn't comment on a little girl's boobs. *Vicki*

> My dad went away for almost a year for work – I was around nine when he got back. The day he returned, I remember him saying to me, "WOW! You've got so skinny!" He always struggled with his weight and he meant it as a compliment. But that comment stayed with me for a long time. Many years later I realized that those words – among other things – had contributed to my belief that being skinny was virtuous and something to aspire to. It took a lot of work to dismantle the resulting body image issues I developed. *Penny*

Conversations with my dad were quite uncomfortable. I remember him saying, "Don't worry, more than a mouthful is a waste!" At the time it made me feel weird and now as an adult, I think it's a weird thing to say. I do remember my dad saying, "No, no, you've got a couple of fried eggs there!" He was teasing me, but it didn't make me feel good. I generally don't find my dad creepy and we have a great relationship – but these comments did not make me feel better in the way he may have meant them to. *Anonymous*

When I got my first swimsuit that wasn't a rash guard and shorts, my dad complimented me. I remember thinking that was gross that he said I looked good in it – just thinking, 'NO.' And I remember sucking in my tummy and looking in the bathroom mirror and thinking, 'What did Dad see that made him want to say that?' *Dee Dee, 16*

It was taboo for my stepdad to talk about breasts or bras. It was like, 'They don't exist!' *Valasca*

When someone drops a clanger, most of the time they haven't thought it through, or didn't know it would hurt. Lots of adults still remember the clangers that badly affected them when they were teenagers.

I was talking about how I had chubby cheeks and my friend said, "You look like a chipmunk who ate too much birthday cake!" And I was like, "OH MY GOD THIS IS WHAT PEOPLE THINK ABOUT ME?" and I absolutely hated my body for all of primary school after that. *Amy, 13*

While there's no way to make yourself immune to a bad comment, you CAN know that these comments happen, and they're stupid, annoying and hurtful.

The best thing you can do is try not to stew on what was said. Sweep it out of your brain and try to replace it with happier, more positive thoughts.

If you want to respond, you could try saying something like, 'Wow, that was a weird/rude thing to say,' with a confused look on your face. That will send a clear message to the person that they've been inappropriate, and you might even get an apology out of them.

People should think harder about what they say and offer compliments, try and empower other people instead of bringing them down. *Edie, 13*

IF IT HELPS, GET SOMEONE YOU TRUST TO SHOW *THIS* PAGE OF THE BOOK TO THE CLANGER-DROPPERS IN YOUR LIFE AND ASK THEM TO PLEASE BE MORE THOUGHTFUL!

A big takeaway I would like to put out – as a man who was once a kid with man boobs, but also just out there in general – is for adults not to body-shame kids. The pre-puberty and adolescent time frame is such a sensitive time for kids and they are so very well attuned to how they look and are perceived by others. Even the slightest difference can lead to waves of embarrassment and self-consciousness. It doesn't take much to do all kinds of damage. *Dan*

Turning self-consciousness into acceptance

What can you do about self-consciousness around your boobs and the rest of your body?

First of all, accept that feeling self-conscious is part of the deal in puberty. It's SO COMMON. Accept that it will pass, too, once you get more familiar with your boobs and they don't feel so new. Just as you might feel self-conscious after a new haircut, sometimes boobs take some getting used to! Then you don't really even think about them that much.

It might also help to ask yourself what values you care about. For instance: kindness! Environmental activism! Equality! Bravery! None of these attributes are affected by a person's appearance.

If I was to give advice to a kid aged eight or nine or ten, I'd say don't get too hung up about the size of your breasts – you never know what they're gonna do! *Catharine Lumby*

Here's some advice from us:

1. **WORK ON YOUR OWN DOUBLE STANDARDS.** If you appreciate courage or cleverness in others, but think you're worthless because of how you look? THAT'S NOT FAIR!

2. **YES, IT IS POSSIBLE TO CHANGE THE WAY YOU LOOK.** People do. Some love it, some regret it. Either way, chances are you're too young to do much more than exercise or dress a certain way to change the way your boobs look, so, for now, changing the way you look isn't a realistic option. ACCEPTANCE, however, IS. And it's a wonderful option!

3. **IDIOTS ARE EVERYWHERE.** A lot of these idiots know that the best way to cut someone down, particularly a woman, and particularly a young woman, is to make her feel bad about her body or appearance. These people are EVERYWHERE and you can't control what they do, but you CAN CONTROL how much you care. So try not to care about what they say! Also, they're jerks, and you shouldn't listen to jerks.

4. **BE A GOOD FRIEND.** Be the person who models body acceptance to her friends. (Be unwavering in this.) Set a good example for those younger than you. Work on expanding what you think is an acceptable body and never pressure anyone to look different from how they look right in this moment. Even if it feels a bit unnatural or fake at first, the more you do it, the more real it will be.

Getting changed for PE/sport

Hesitating about getting changed when you're shy about your breasts is perfectly understandable.

There are ways to take bras off under a T-shirt or jumper – but this is close to impossible if it's a bra without clasps, like a sports bra. It is also extremely difficult to put a bra ON under clothes, although it can be done if it's a bra with clasps.

> If I was twelve and someone told me, "It's part of growing up!" I would want to hit them! Just because it's something that a lot of people experience doesn't make it easier in the moment. There are things you can do to make it more comfortable – covering up with a towel, going to a different space. If you're going to be more comfortable going into a toilet stall, then do it. *Lily, 17*

Sometimes, **you've just got to get changed** – in or out of your bra – in front of other people. If you're really shy about your boobs being seen, the best thing you can do is get changed quickly in a toilet stall or a changing cubicle. Most school groups will be pretty respectful of your need for privacy provided you don't take so long that it inconveniences others.

1. Undo your bra.

2. Pull your arms out of their sleeves, inside your shirt.

3. Unloop your bra straps from your arms.

4. Pull your bra out from under your shirt.

5. Celebrate!

> In Year Eleven one of my friends came back from doing a student exchange in Iceland. They're apparently mad for a bit of communal nudity over there and she was supremely relaxed showering naked in the open while the rest of us were cowering in the corners. *Yumi*

> I have one friend who doesn't like getting changed in front of other people and she goes into the cubicle and everybody just accepts it. *Evie, 13*

> If I'm too uncomfortable, like if there's a lot of people around, I'll turn to face a wall. *Grace, 13*

You might like to plan ahead; see if you can have part of your outfit under your existing clothes so that you just have to take a few key pieces off (for example, you might be able to wear your swimsuit beneath your school uniform). You may need to change into clean clothes afterwards, but this at least reduces the exposure to just one change's worth!

One thing you might notice as you get older is that exposure reduces your sensitivity. In other words, the more you do something awkward, the less dorky you feel doing it. So the more times you change clothes in front of others, the less shy you'll feel about it.

Visiting the doctor

Sometimes the best way to deal with worries about boobs is to see a doctor. You might have a general practitioner (GP) you've known since you were a small kid. You know, the one who gave you your vaccinations, or looks after your asthma or always sees you when you're sick. But when puberty starts, it can feel super awkward going to the doctor to talk about boobs! Maybe you don't have a regular GP and don't know who to see. Most young teens rely on, and are happy for, their parents or carers

> When I was answering questions in *Dolly* magazine from young teens about puberty, many of them said to me '... and I don't want to see the doctor!' *Dr Melissa*

to help them get to a doctor. It can be hard to know how to make an appointment or figure out if it will cost money. But if you can't involve a parent for whatever reason, you still have the right to see a doctor, even if it's on your own. You can try to find an adult, or older sibling, who can help. The NHS website (or the HSE Service Finder Map in Ireland) can help you find a GP near you.

The doctor rarely needs to see you topless ...

Self-consciousness is a natural feeling for many teens going through puberty. The thought of talking to a doctor, and especially being examined by them, can feel super awkward at this stage of life.

A doctor might want to examine you if you have a cough, chest pains, asthma or flu symptoms. Sometimes they might want to listen to your heart by using a stethoscope over the front of your chest. If you have tummy pains or gastro symptoms, they might want to check your abdomen, including the upper part towards your chest. Other scenarios, like examining a rash or pimples over your back, checking your spine, ribs and shoulders, can mean the doctor will want to look at your whole torso.

> I have to get back check-ups sometimes but normally they let me leave my bra on. When I was younger I didn't wear one and I didn't really mind. Even when I was younger they would always ask permission – "Is it OK if you take your shirt off?" They warn me, 'I'm going to touch you on the back.' *Edie, 13*

In any of these circumstances, your doctor should be able to examine your chest without you having to remove your clothes (unless it's an outer jacket, hoodie etc.). They might ask you to lift a T-shirt or singlet up to look at your skin or to place the stethoscope around the chest. You should not have to remove your bra.

If your symptoms or worries are about your boobs, it doesn't necessarily mean the doctor needs to examine them. A lot of information can come just from your description of your concerns and symptoms. If you're wanting advice about whether your boobs are developing normally, the doctor can show you a diagram of the five stages of boob development and ask you to point out where you're at.

MORE ON p. 12

... but once in a while, the doctor does need to see you with your top off.

Sometimes, though, it is going to be helpful if a doctor examines your boobs. It might be because of a rash, pain or a lump. As confronting as that seems, it's what doctors are trained to do: they examine people's body parts all the time. They're used to it!

Here are some facts and tips about being examined by a doctor:

- **A doctor can only examine you if you give permission.**
- **You have the right to say no to an examination.**
- **You have the right to ask for a doctor of a gender of your choice and to wait until one is available.**
- **You can ask a doctor to explain what they are going to do and why – before they examine you.**
- **You can have someone else in the room (such as a parent or friend) if you wish.**
- **Doctors examine people all the time – examining the chest, tummy, boobs or any other part of the body is routine for them.**
- **Doctors don't feel awkward about examining people, but are very keen to make sure you feel comfortable.**
- **If you're visiting a doctor and think they might need to examine your chest, you might feel more comfortable wearing a crop top or sports bra.**
- **You have the right to call 'stop' at any time, and you can forewarn them by saying, "This makes me uncomfortable and I would like it to go as quickly as possible." Or, "I'm just warning you that I may call STOP."**
- **It can take a while (maybe two or three visits) to feel comfortable talking to a doctor – you will know if a doctor is right for you. If they're not, you can bail on them and look for a doctor you do like.**

BOOBS AND THE REST OF MY BODY

Breast changes over the menstrual cycle

They definitely change size and firmness depending on what time of the month it is (in relation to my menstrual cycle). They might look saggier and less full, depending on the time of the month – usually the week of menstruation. *Nadia*

Boobs start growing very early in puberty, when breast buds appear.

MORE ON p. 12

On average it's **two years** from the appearance of those breast buds before the first period comes. From then it can take another one to two years to establish a predictable period 'cycle'.

Boobs grow because of hormones called oestrogen and progesterone, and these hormones also totally OWN the menstrual cycle. There's a LOT going on with hormones! Their levels go up and down each month, fine-tuning what happens inside the ovaries, uterus (internal reproductive organs) and boobs. This is your body's way of practising for making babies, even if that doesn't happen for many years or, like – ever.

Oestrogen makes the ducts (tiny tubes) in breast tissue enlarge, and progesterone makes the milk-producing cells swell. A lot of people don't notice any changes, but for some they will feel and see their boobs swell up – usually just before a period – and then go down again.

Breast side effects from the Pill/contraception/other medications

There are now very safe and effective medications for teens and young people to avoid pregnancy or to deal with painful or heavy periods. These are known as hormonal contraceptives, since they contain small amounts of hormones and prevent pregnancy. They come in the form of pills (often called 'the Pill'), an implant (often called 'the rod', which goes under the skin in the arm), a tiny plastic device that goes inside the uterus (called an 'IUD') or an injection in the butt. These medications can mimic what happens in the menstrual cycle, meaning that boobs can grow and swell a little. But these side effects don't usually last.

Boobs and sex! Getting turned on

Boobs have an important part to play when it comes to sex. For some people, boobs and nipples are the most sexually sensitive part of the body after the genitals. For other people, their nipples are so sensitive that almost all touch is painful, and they prefer any sexual play to avoid the nipple itself. It's normal and safe to touch your own nipples and enjoy the sensation or to explore what feels good, bad or indifferent. Nipple sensitivity can fluctuate – sometimes with the menstrual cycle, possibly with your moods, or for no reason at all.

MORE ON p. 160

Looking after my boobs – checking boobs, nipple care, skin care

Every part of our body is worth taking good care of – it's got to see us through! Boobs deserve a special mention, though, because they **change** so much over time. The hormones of puberty, pregnancy and breastfeeding cause drastic changes to their size, shape and function. Medications (including some contraceptives) might affect how they look and feel. And sometimes boobs get sick and need help.

> I always say that your body is like a car: you drive it till you die, and you don't ever get to trade it in for a new one! So we have to love our bodies and maintain them – treat your body like the car you want to last for LIFE. Because it's the only one you get! *Yumi*

MORE ON p. 163

Boobs are also pretty resilient. They can handle a fair bit of physical activity or getting bumped while playing sports. If you're super active or do lots of contact sports, it's worth wearing a firm sports bra. It not only feels more comfortable, but helps to minimise soft-tissue bruising from an accidental whack from a fast-moving ball, frisbee, elbow or knee!

Looking after your nipples, areolae and the skin covering your boobs is also important. Standard skin care, such as avoiding sunburn (that means wearing sunscreen on any exposed skin) and drinking plenty of water are usually enough to take care of teen boobs. If you are breastfeeding, your nipples will need extra care.

MORE ON p. 199

You might also have heard about checking your boobs regularly for lumps. The technical expression for this is 'breast self-examination' (BSE), which is exactly what it sounds like. It's a step-by-step routine for looking at and feeling the tissues in your boobs about once a month, to check for changes or lumps. Getting the hang of breast self-examination from a young age is good for your future boob health, but it also helps you get to know your boobs and feel comfortable with them. There are apps you can put on your smartphone that remind you when you're due for a self-examination, show you techniques and are actually pretty fun.

Here are some tips for breast self-examination to remember for the rest of your life.

It's recommended that you do BSE just after your period is finished. It's when your boobs are least likely to be sore or swollen from period hormones.

JUST TO REASSURE YOU, BREAST CANCER IN TEENS IS EXTREMELY UNLIKELY. OTHER LUMPS CAN OCCUR THAT ARE NOT CANCER BUT MIGHT NEED SOME MEDICAL ATTENTION.

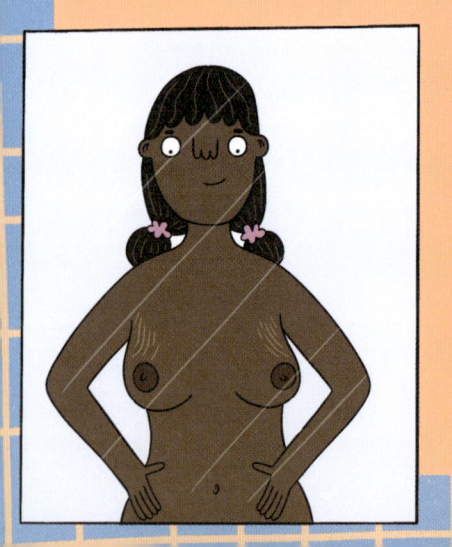

LOOK FIRST:

★ Take off your top and bra. Face the mirror directly and put your hands on your hips.

☆ Push your shoulders forward to tense your chest muscles.

★ Get to know which boob hangs lower, and what your nipples, areolae and skin look like.

Then **feel**. Hold your fingers together like you would in a karate chop! Use this flat part of your held-together fingers to feel your boob. It's easiest to use your right hand to feel your left boob, and left hand to feel your right boob. Starting in one part of your boob, go around in a circle and up into your armpit. Remember that boob tissue goes up into each armpit. You'll notice whether your boobs naturally feel soft, squishy or lumpy. Feel under the nipple too.

Doing BSE in the shower is often an easy way to look after your boobs while getting clean. But you might prefer to examine your boobs while lying down. Either or both is fine.

What you're looking for is any kind of change. A new lump or bump? A change in the skin on your nipples or boobs? Follow up anything out of the ordinary with your doctor as soon as you can – even if it's nothing, you'll feel better for knowing!

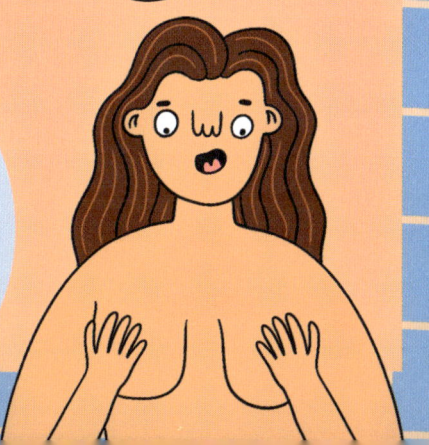

PUBES GO WITH BOOBS!

> Yes. It's true!

Around the same time as your boobs start to bud, you might also notice a light growth of hair appearing on your genital area. As time passes, it will thicken into a full thatch of pubes. Most commonly, pubic hair – aka pubes – will start to show a couple of weeks or months later than when your breast buds appear. Sometimes they appear before or at the same time. It's all normal.

> When? ... NOW?

Pubes can arrive any time from when you're eight years old (for girls) or nine years old (for boys). In boys, pubes appear just after, just before, or around the same time as the testes ('balls') start to grow. (Their balls were always there, but their size increases about six-fold by the end of puberty.)

In girls, pubic hair grows on the outer lips (outer 'labia') of the vulva and across the spongy pad of skin in front of the pubic bone. These little hairs can also grow out to the inside of the upper thighs and near the anus, or bum hole.

When pubic hairs first appear, they're usually quite soft and downy. By the end of puberty, they are thicker and more curly or wiry compared to the hair on your head or other parts of your body. It's common for pubic hair to be a different colour to head hair – usually darker. The best predictor of what colour your pubes will be is your eyebrows! But that's not 100 per cent guaranteed.

The five stages of pube growth

STAGE 1: The hair on the vulva is tiny, and barely visible.

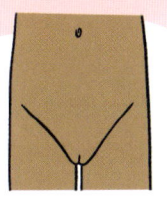

STAGE 2: Hairs become visible on each of the outer labia. Each hair is slightly darker and thicker than before. More and more hairs appear on each side.

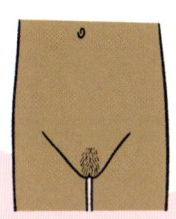

STAGE 3: Growth of your pubic hair has extended up to the top of the outer labia (lips) and meets in the middle in front of the pubic bone. The individual hairs have become thicker.

STAGE 4: Your pubic hair covers the area like an upside-down triangle. The hairs are thicker, and curly or wiry.

STAGE 5: Pubes are fully grown and extend out towards the thighs and down around your butthole.

FUN FACT: ADULT PUBES USUALLY GROW BETWEEN 2.5CM TO 3.8CM BEFORE THEY FALL OUT.

What the heck are these hairs for?

Pubes indicate biological readiness for reproduction. They also indicate you're in puberty!

Pubes create a buffer between your undies and the skin on your private parts. This helps regulate your temperature and also allows for airflow, so your vulva can breathe! (Vulvas love air.)

Pubes reduce friction on the sensitive skin underneath them. This is meaningful when you're doing any kind of physical activity, like exercise, and comes in handy when you're older and having sex. People mistakenly think removing pubes reduces friction, but hair-on-hair activity actually creates a lot less friction than skin-on-skin activity.

Pubes filter dirt and other bacteria from getting into your body through your vagina – just like your eyelashes do for your eyes! Your whole vagina and vulva has its own ecosystem of microorganisms (a 'microbiome'), which is self-cleaning. It keeps acidity levels healthy and helps prevent 'bad' bacteria from causing infections. Pubes are the outer layer of protection.

Discharge

The secretions you'll see on your undies is part of this self-cleaning system too. Discharge is perfectly normal and part of the bigger change that's going on with your body. It first appears about twelve to eighteen months after your boobs first bud and there's more and more of it as you head towards your first period. It's about lubrication, which helps your body to move around comfortably. At this stage, it's also signalling to you that you have a vagina! This is not the whole genitalia that sits inside your undies (that's the vulva). The vagina is the muscular passage that leads from the outside world to your uterus. From it will come menstrual fluid, and from it comes discharge. Pubes tend to stop a lot of it from ending up on your underwear.

Are pubes dirty? How do I keep them clean?

Nope! Pubes are not dirty. But they do trap smells known as 'pheromones' which, theoretically, can increase how attractive we are to potential sex partners. And that's just part of our human smell.

Keep them clean with warm water when you wash! Anything too soapy could hurt your vaginal microbiome, so go easy on the soaps and shampoos.

Can I trim?

Yep! We're not enthusiastic about pubic hair removal, but a little trim with safety scissors is okay. Be careful, though! The skin that covers your genitals is sensitive – be gentle with it. Removing pubes by shaving, hair removal creams or waxing can come with hellacious itching, ingrown hairs and rashes. Trimming or removing pubes is a personal choice – and no-one's business but yours.

BOOB MYTHS

There are some myths about boobs that persist, even with so much reliable, scientific evidence that they are NOT TRUE! Here are a few of them:

Eating chicken causes early boob development

FALSE!

All my cousins, aunts and uncles – they all used to talk about how I must eat chicken! I wasn't fat but I was chunky and I had boobs, so I thought it was the chicken! Because that's what all the adults were saying! *Skylar, 23*

I had heard that eating chicken makes your boobs grow but I didn't believe it – I was just like, ALL RIGHT. BELIEVE WHAT YOU WANT TO BELIEVE. *Gracie N, 14*

The myth goes something like this: chickens are given hormones to make them grow faster. Children eat the chicken and get a dose of those hormones, causing their boobs to grow much earlier than they would otherwise. There are at least two reasons why this isn't true.

For starters, in the UK and Ireland there are laws that prohibit the use of growth hormones in chickens. And second, even if it did happen, cooking chicken meat would deactivate the hormones. (And eating raw chicken is definitely **not** a thing – it would make you very sick!)

Endocrine disruptors make boobs develop early — NOT SURE

Scientists and doctors have noticed in the past generation or so that boobs MIGHT be developing at a younger age. Other aspects of puberty, such as when you get your first period, haven't really changed in almost a hundred years. There's now scientific evidence that certain chemicals as well as naturally occurring substances could be responsible for earlier boob development. These chemicals and substances are called endocrine disruptors because they might block or change some of the body's hormone actions. Hormones form part of the body's endocrine system. The biggest culprit is certain plastics that contain those chemicals, including plastic used in making food containers. The list also includes some of the chemicals used in cosmetics and perfumes. It's likely that the existence of these chemicals alone isn't going to make your boobs suddenly grow – otherwise we'd be seeing boobs everywhere. Some scientists think that the chemicals might get released when, say, a plastic container with food in it is heated. It's a case of watch this space – but in the meantime some puberty experts (and climate activists!) are saying it's good to discourage the use of certain plastics.

Exercising can make your boobs grow — FALSE!

A hilarious myth that went around when we were kids was that you could increase the size of your boobs by exercising and chanting! The exercise was flapping your elbows backwards and forwards over and over while repeating, 'I must, I must, I must increase my bust!'

Breasts are made up mostly of fat tissue, and you can't tone fat with exercise. You can only lose it – that is, reduce size – or strengthen the muscles around your chest to create the illusion of size and lift.

ON REFLECTION, IT SEEMS UNLIKELY ANYONE TRULY BELIEVED IT WOULD WORK, AND IT WAS MORE ABOUT FEMALE BONDING: A FUNNY THING TO DO WITH YOUR MATES, WHILE LAUGHING YOUR BUTTS OFF.

> I heard that if you wear a bra in bed it makes them saggy! I'm not sure if that's true or not. *Gracie N. 14*

Wearing a bra at night gives you breast cancer — **FALSE!**

Another myth you might've heard is that it's bad to wear a bra to bed and while sleeping. Yeah, nah. Wearing any clothing that is too tight can be uncomfortable and leave you with band marks the next day. But it won't do any harm, won't cause sag, and absolutely definitely won't give you cancer. That goes for underwire bras, crop tops, t-shirt bras, or anything at all. Wearing a bra that helps you feel comfortable while you sleep is perfectly OK. As a general rule, if it feels cosy and not tight, it is fine.

Sleeping on your boobs stops them from growing

FALSE!

Sleeping on your boobs in no way affects their growth. The best way to sleep for boob health is whatever way feels most comfortable for you.

> The first bra I got was a crop top. I was so excited I wore it to bed that night! *Clem, 39*

> I usually sleep on my side – my boobs are not a problem. My partner has small boobs and sometimes when I roll over I accidentally pin them down and that hurts her! *Laura*

Sleeping with your phone in your bedroom at night gives you breast cancer

FALSE!

There is **no link** with breast cancer in any of the research that's been done on mobile phones and cancer. Mobile phones (cell phones, hand phones, digital phones) work by using something called radiofrequency radiation. Different types of

> I'm a very superstitious person. So I know it's not true but I can't get it out of my head – so JUST IN CASE I deliberately don't keep my phone in my room overnight. *Olive, 14*

radiofrequency radiation are used in television and radio broadcasting, Wi-fi, bluetooth and plenty of other everyday devices, including 5G networks. The Earth, sun and sky also emit natural forms of radiofrequency radiation. Radiofrequency radiation is generally safe.

Because mobile phones are held close to the head when people talk on them, scientists and researchers have studied them for many years to see whether there is an increased risk for people to develop brain tumours. Important health and cancer authorities in the UK and Ireland and overseas currently say that there is no clear link between mobile phone use and cancer, including in children. Research is ongoing, since technology keeps changing. Authorities recommend keeping mobile phones further away from the head when using them (by using headphones, speakers, etc.), as that further reduces the amount of radiation that reaches the brain (or anywhere else in the body). Earbuds that use bluetooth are massively on the rise, and these are also thought to be safe.

Nonetheless, lots of teens are reporting that their parents tell them sleeping with their mobile phone in their bedrooms could give them breast cancer!

> HAVING A MOBILE PHONE IN YOUR BEDROOM IS SAFE FROM A CANCER POINT OF VIEW – BREAST, BRAIN OR OTHERWISE.

The likely story is that parents are repeating this myth because they want to discourage phone addiction and late-night scrolling. (And that is actually a pretty good idea! Sorry ... but also not sorry.)

Boobs are an erogenous zone for all women — FALSE!

An 'erogenous' part of the body is anywhere that is sensitive to sexual stimulation. There is a strongly held myth that boobs are an erogenous zone for everyone, especially women.

While some people like it or love it, and others are indifferent to it, a lot of people really **don't like** having their boobs touched. In particular, they don't like having their nipples touched. This includes during sex or intimate contact. Their nipples are too sensitive for them to enjoy it and it can be the opposite of sexy: a turn-off. So before you touch anyone's boobs, it's always a good idea to ask – and make sure you're asked in return!

> I like to have them touched but not kissed or sucked. *Claire, 40*

> Boobs have never been an erogenous zone for me. That's been a bit of a bugbear of mine because people I've been in sexual relationships with have assumed that that's an erogenous zone, and for me it's not. *Valasca*

> It's fine if they ask first and it's a gay guy or a female friend – I actually don't mind most times. But in sexual situations with the opposite sex, I don't really like it. *Anouk, 18*

> I hate having my boobs touched so much! Even with a partner, I don't really like it. Guys think it's desired for them to do that, but NO. I like touching other people's boobs but I don't like mine being touched! *Dee Dee, 16*

> Everyone is brought up to think women's breasts are erogenous – you kind of have to unlearn that as you grow up, and it comes from straight men sexualizing women. Because they like boobs and therefore assume women must like straight men giving them attention. *Skylar, 23*

You can stop your boobs from sagging

SORT OF BUT NOT REALLY

Boobs might sag over time because of genetics, size, age and gravity. Sagging can also be caused by the stretching and emptying of the boob that can occur with weight gain and loss, including (and especially) during pregnancy. It's not a bad thing at all – it's just part of life. It happens when the Cooper's ligaments that support your breasts stretch over time (in fact, it's sometimes also called droop or Cooper's droop). Once stretched, these ligaments can't go back to their original form.

MORE ON p. 66

The science is out on just how much wearing a bra during the day helps to prevent sag, but there is an agreement that excessive bounce during exercise can stretch the Cooper's ligaments. Therefore, wearing a well-fitting sports bra during exercise is a good idea if you want to prevent sag (and also pain). Wearing a bra at night-time will not prevent sag, though.

If you don't like the way your boobs look when they sag, there's a really mainstream way to fix it. Guess what it is …? A bra!

JUST REMEMBER: BOOBS CAN BE GOOD-LOOKING NO MATTER WHERE THEY SIT! IT'S ALL ABOUT PERSPECTIVE.

IS SOMETHING WRONG?

Lumps and bumps, scary, hairy or scratchy nipples, or aches, pains and discharge are some of the things that happen to boobs. Most of them are nothing to worry about, even if they're uncomfortable. But, like any part of the body, boobs sometimes aren't quite right and need medical attention.

All of the scenarios below deserve a check-up by a doctor who you trust and feel comfortable with. Often it's for reassurance, but sometimes a doctor will recommend some tests, such as blood tests or an ultrasound. Yes, it can be tricky seeing a doctor when you're young – but, like getting your driver's licence and (gasp!) wearing a bra, seeing a doctor by yourself is a grown-up thing that you will eventually be doing on your own. Like, maybe … now? Or soon? The section Visiting the Doctor, on page 141, explains why it can feel awkward, and things you might want to know when talking to a doctor about your boobs.

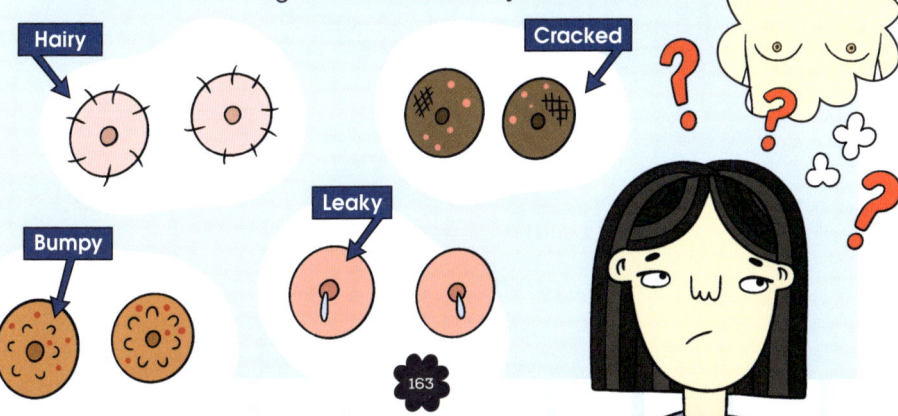

Lumps

Hairy

Cracked

Bumpy

Leaky

It's completely up to you whether you want to have an adult in the room with you when you go to see the doctor. Adolescent health experts around the world encourage doctors to spend time talking with teens without a parent in the room – unless having one present is the clear preference of the teen – to make sure they're able to give them the best possible care. Sometimes a teen can feel more open if they talk to a doctor by themselves. It's often still helpful for parents and carers to be involved so doctors can ask for their perspective as well. (The adult may remember details the teen has forgotten, or know the family history.) So even if the teen's adult doesn't stay for the whole appointment, they might spend a few minutes chatting all together before or after the session.

Phonecall appointments may make this easier, and not needing to show up in person mean you can even do the call from school if needed. If you get nervous before you talk to your doctor, it can help to write a few things down – all your key questions, all the important things you want to tell them.

> Sometimes my daughter freezes up at the doctor's, so often I go in with her, make sure she has communicated the essential information, then I ask if she wants me to leave. She usually says yes, so I wait out in the waiting room – respecting her privacy but also there if she needs help. *Yumi*

Hairy boobs

Areolae, those darker circles around the nipples, have a small number of hair follicles sitting towards the edges where they join the skin. They hang around during childhood, ready to spring into action when your boobs develop during puberty. These hairs resemble pubic hair – they're thick and a bit wiry. If you've noticed a few nipple hairs as your boobs grow, it's usually a sign that your puberty hormones are doing their job.

Sometimes a hormone imbalance will set off more hair growth – one minute there are two or three hairs on each boob, and the next it's double or triple. Increased body and facial hair happen to everyone in puberty, but much less in females than males. So, if you think you have hairier-than-normal boobs, look out for other areas of hair growth that are unusual in biological females – such as in the middle of your chest between your boobs, or across your lower abdomen and pelvic area. The most common cause of this pattern of hairiness in females is a condition called polycystic ovarian syndrome. This condition also commonly causes irregular periods and acne. It can be associated with weight issues, especially being overweight or having difficulty losing weight. Hairy boobs might also be caused by the use of some medication, some other hormone or a medical condition.

Lumps

MORE ON p. 63

There are lumpy boobs and then there are lumps in boobs that weren't there before. In people under twenty years old this is almost never cancer.

A 'breast mouse'

The most common breast lump in teens is something called a fibroadenoma. It happens in about one in fifty female teens and is benign, meaning it is NOT cancer. Also, having one of these does NOT increase your chances of getting breast cancer.

If you get a fibroadenoma, it will usually grow only in one breast, not both, and it usually appears in the top half of the breast towards the outer edge. They can be a few millimetres in diameter up to a couple of centimetres. Rarely, they grow as large as five centimetres in diameter. These lumps can change in size with the menstrual cycle, usually swelling up a bit just before your period and then going back down again once your period starts.

They are quite slippery! One moment you feel the lump between your fingers and the next, it has slipped away. Fibroadenomas have been called 'breast mice' by doctors

Fibroadenoma

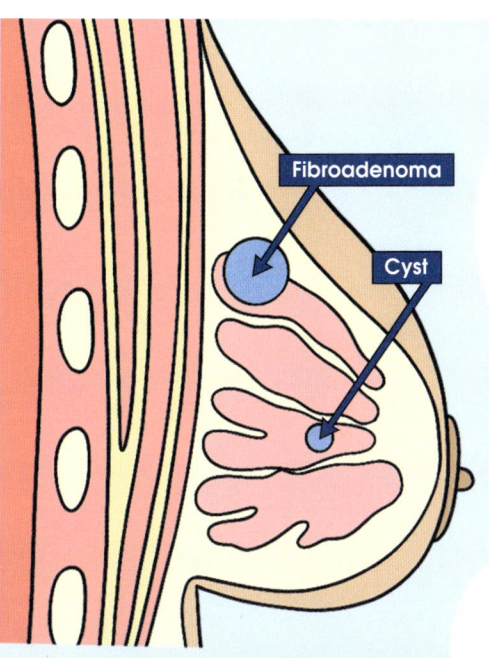

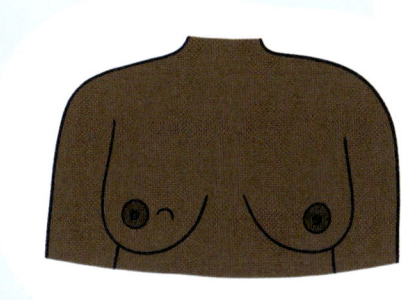

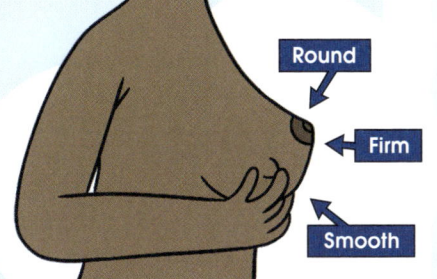

Cyst

Round

Firm

Smooth

because they 'run away' from the person examining them.

To confirm that the lump is a fibroadenoma, your doctor would order a breast ultrasound to look at the texture and size of the lump, and might also ask for a **biopsy**. And then, after a few years, mostly they just shrink away and disappear. Or not. If they get really big, they can be removed by a breast surgeon.

MORE ON p. 168

WHAT DO YOU MEAN, BIOPSY??

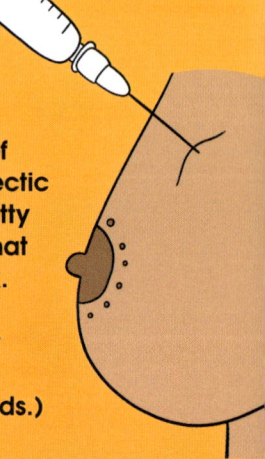

A biopsy means a tiny needle is inserted into the lump to take out some cells and confirm the type of tissue it is. I hear you freaking out! It sounds a bit hectic – but if there's any pain it's short-lived and, TBH, pretty minimal. Very often it is an extremely thin needle that takes the biopsy – so thin it's like the tiniest pinprick. The doctor can also inject a local anaesthetic to completely numb the skin and tissues, so you don't actually feel anything. (Injecting the anaesthetic stings a tiny bit, but it goes numb within sixty seconds.)

What's a mammogram and do I need one?

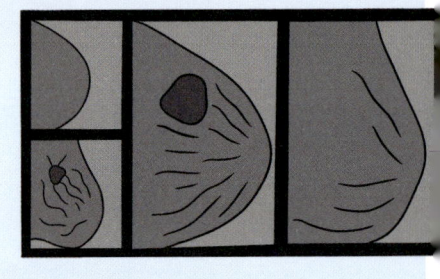

A mammogram is literally an X-ray of the breast. Yep – the same thing as having an X-ray to see if you fractured your ankle or your wrist, only this one looks at the breast.

Mammograms are generally NOT a good test in teenagers who have a lump or lumpiness of the breasts – ultrasounds are the way to go. This is because of what's going on inside a puberty boob and the causes of breast

MORE ON p. 10

MORE ON p. 166

lumps in teens – they are easier and more accurate to diagnose with an ultrasound.

For later in life, mammograms are one of the key ways that breast cancer is detected. Breast cancer is more common in women over 50. To get a clear picture of what's going on inside your breast, your boob is sandwiched between two plates for a few seconds while a tech takes the pictures. Getting your boob squished hard like this is actually the opposite of fun and you are totally allowed to complain and plan for, like, reward doughnuts afterwards if you want!
But it's over pretty quickly. Usually two pictures per breast are taken.

Here are some reasons why an adult over 35 years old might get a mammogram. If you're under 35 years old, you might be referred for an ultrasound with these symptoms.

IN THE UK, ANYONE REGISTERED WITH A GP AS FEMALE WILL BE INVITED FOR NHS BREAST SCREENING EVERY 3 YEARS (2 IN IRELAND) BETWEEN THE AGES OF 50 AND 71. (50 AND 69 IN IRELAND)

Dimples

Breast skin change

Nipple retraction

Nipple discharge

Breast cysts

A 'cyst' is a sac inside the body that is filled with fluid. Think of a (teeny-tiny) mini water balloon. A breast cyst usually grows out of the milk-making breast tissue that develops during puberty. This tissue is influenced by the hormones of the menstrual cycle. So, once you start having periods, little cysts might form or swell up and then go down again during your cycle. Sometimes the cyst swells up and doesn't go down again, and you might feel it as a soft – or even a firm (but not hard) – lump. Cysts can also be a bit tender.

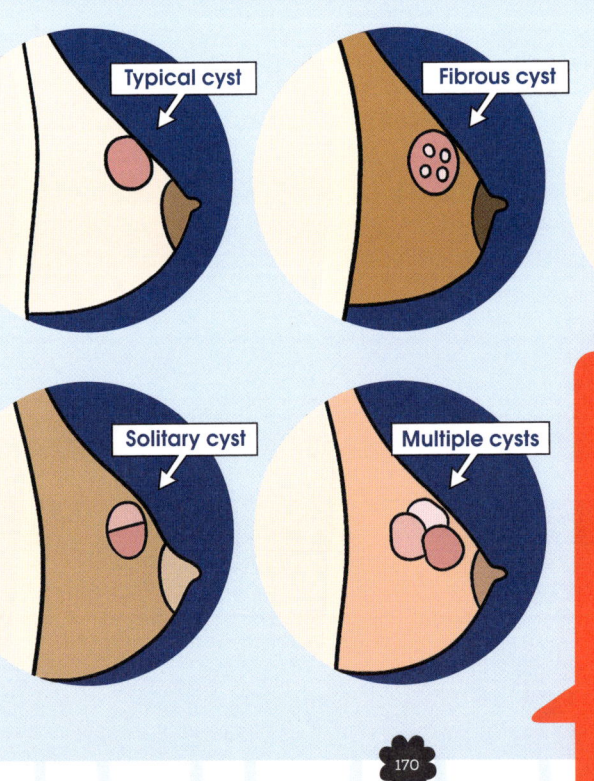

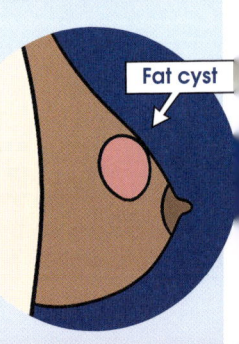

Typical cyst

Fibrous cyst

Fat cyst

Solitary cyst

Multiple cysts

> I was about forty and had a lot of soreness. My doctor was concerned so I went for a biopsy and they found a bunch more cysts that I wasn't even aware of. Thankfully they were all benign and I just have lumpy boobs. What a relief! *Lorna*

Most cysts don't need any treatment and will often go away on their own. If they hurt, doctors recommend taking pain medication similar to what you'd use for period pain, and wearing the most comfortable bra possible!

Growing pain

Boobs can be intermittently sore and tender when they're growing. Although unpleasant, this is considered common and normal as new tissues grow larger and your skin gets stretched.

> Halfway through last year my boobs started to grow. It kind of hurt a little bit, not that much, but you could just feel them and you could see the difference. *Grace, 13*

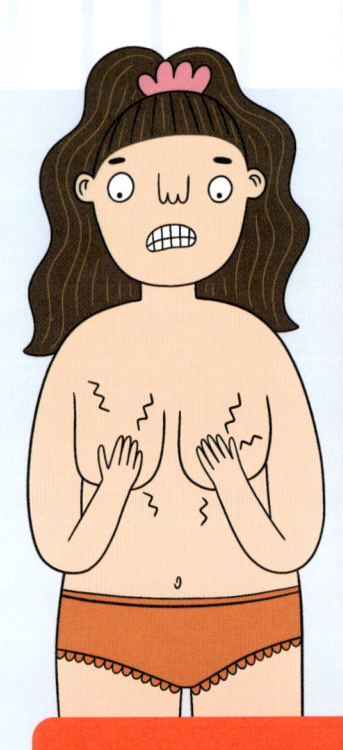

I was about elven, twelve, and I started growing them when I just started puberty – I started getting pain in THAT area and they started popping up, coming out, you know? It kind of hurt until I got to a proper size. It wasn't a constant pain – a few times a month or something it would just start hurting. And then the pain went away in Year Seven and they just kind of grew themselves and I didn't really feel it. *Holly, 15*

There was pain when my boobs started growing – tenderness! I told my mum, but mostly me and my twin sister spoke about it. I was in a big hurry to grow up, so I was very excited! *Laura*

Cyclical pain

Once periods start, some people get 'cyclical' pain in their boobs. It means that pain comes and goes at **specific times in the menstrual cycle.** Around 70 per cent of people will experience this. (Translation: that's a LOT of us.) In the few days leading up to a period, boobs can swell up and feel sore, and this goes away once the period starts.

> There are these parts of my body that are making my life difficult every month! *Lily, 17*

> The only problem I have is right before my period when my boobs hurt pretty bad. *Anouk, 18*

Boob pain caused by menstrual cycle hormones usually affects both breasts, and soreness is felt within the whole breast and even up to the armpits. It can be mild, moderate or severe, where boobs are sore to touch or bump. Some people have 'fibrocystic' boobs, which can be more prone to soreness and pain before a period.

MORE ON p. 64

> The week before my period, they are sore and full and DON'T YOU DARE TOUCH. If someone accidentally elbows me (which happens cos they're sticking out) – oooooh, the pain! *Berno*

There is an over-the-counter gel called diclofenac which has been found to relieve this kind of pain. Over-the-counter pain tablets might also help, and so can wearing supportive bras. Sometimes period cycle-related pain does become regular or severe enough to be assessed by your doctor. It's important to get the diagnosis right and look at options such as prescription medications.

Other sources of pain

Sometimes boob pain is not related to your period cycle. It can be due to something that's **not** in your boob – such as a sprain in the chest muscles or ribs underneath or very close to where your boobs are. Injuries to the boob can also cause pain (a whack to the boob from a flying football, for example). People with big boobs may also get discomfort or pain because of strain on the ligaments that attach the breasts to the chest.

Infections of the skin and tissues just underneath the skin can also cause a lot of pain – usually accompanied by red, hot skin. These might come about from a scratch or an insect bite in the skin, although it's rare that such an infection would take hold unless you've had recent surgery there or have a health condition that might affect your immune system.

Mastitis is inflammation of the breast tissues and milk glands themselves and can be super painful. It's caused by

Healthy breast

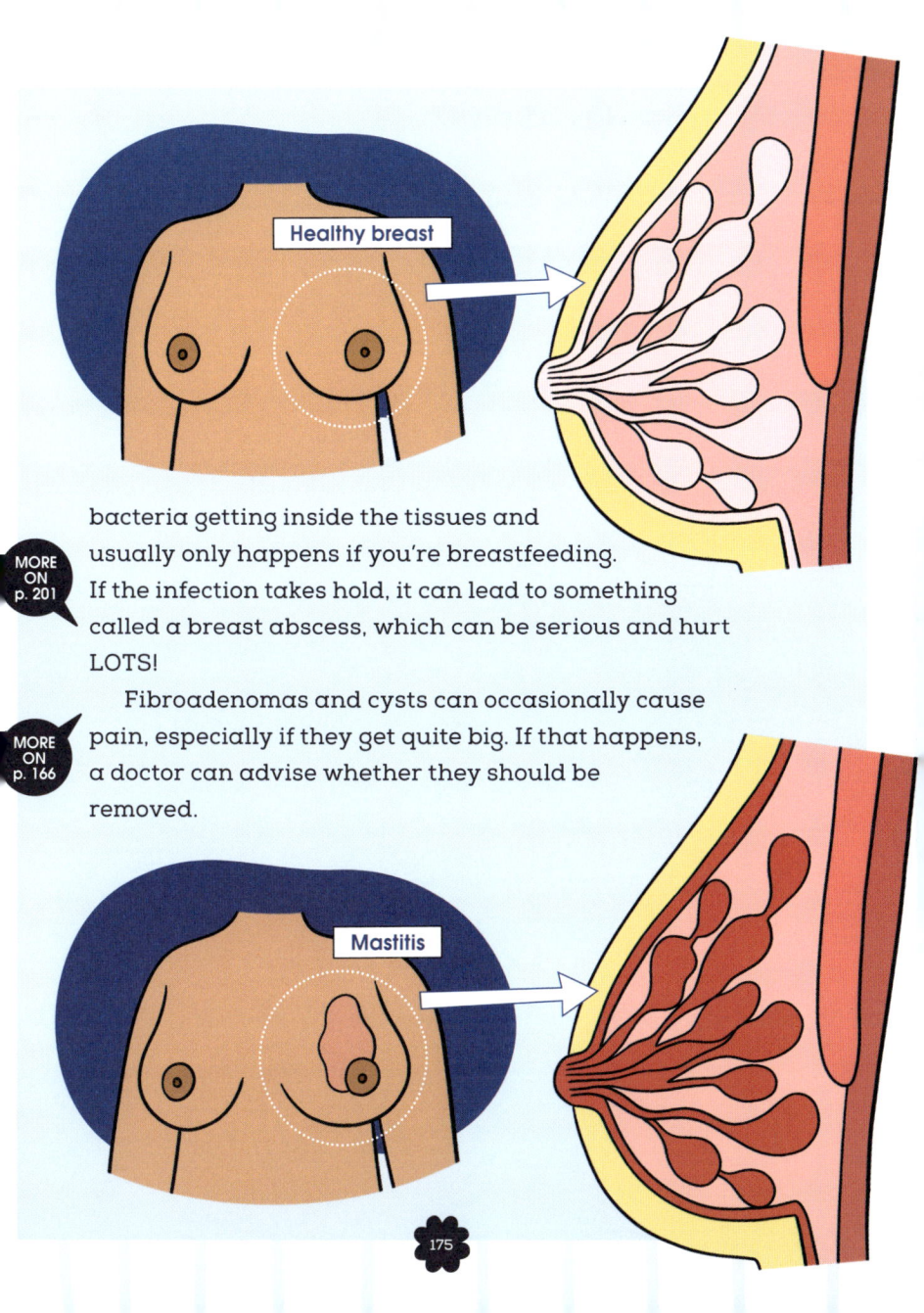

bacteria getting inside the tissues and usually only happens if you're breastfeeding. If the infection takes hold, it can lead to something called a breast abscess, which can be serious and hurt LOTS!

Fibroadenomas and cysts can occasionally cause pain, especially if they get quite big. If that happens, a doctor can advise whether they should be removed.

MORE ON p. 201

MORE ON p. 166

Mastitis

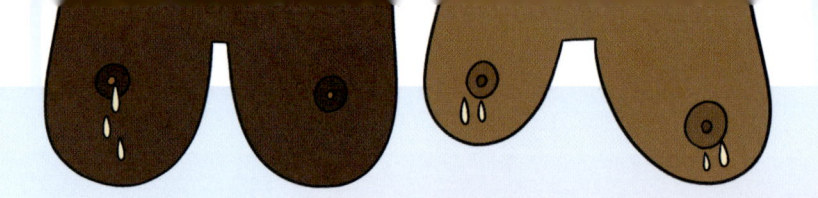

Discharge

> On the areola there'll be tiny little areas where you can squeeze a little bit of secretion out – milky white. It's never been something that bothered me. It doesn't come out of the nipple, it comes out of a spot around the nipple that's not a pimple. More like a pore that contains oil, but is not inflamed. *Clem, 39*

There's nothing to be worried about if you discover an oily or waxy substance coming from the areola. It's coming from the Montgomery glands and is usually a small, unnoticeable amount. Its purpose is to moisturise and protect your nipple.

MORE ON p. 65

Nipple discharge, or, why is MILK coming from my nipple when I haven't had a baby?

First, make sure you're not confusing nipple discharge with the Montgomery gland secretion mentioned earlier. That secretion's texture is quite waxy and very normal.

Puberty nipples can leak a clear, yellow, grey or white discharge as a result of squeezing or rubbing them. It happens because of a hormone called prolactin. Prolactin actually causes breast tissues to make milk – usually after a pregnancy. A complex chain of hormone reactions allows this to happen. If you haven't been pregnant but there seems to be milk or clear fluid coming out of the nipples, it's a good idea to have your prolactin levels checked. Perhaps there's been some prolactin excess due to an overgrowth of cells that make prolactin (called a prolactinoma), a hormonal imbalance, a medication side effect, or even stress.

When I was 18, I was diagnosed with hyperprolactinemia. It's where your body has more prolactin than usual – that's the hormone that tells the breast to make milk. When you're pregnant or breastfeeding, this hormone production is switched on, but not if you're a never-been-pregnant 18-year-old! There were times when breast milk literally sprayed out of my breast, occasionally at very inappropriate times! I had an MRI when I was diagnosed and then I had another one about two years ago and both came clear so they actually have no idea why I have it. *Alex, 36*

Otherwise, there are a couple of uncommon causes of nipple discharge, which can be clear, yellow or blood-stained, in teens. The first is a small growth inside the nipple called a papilloma. Another cause is duct ectasia, which is when the tubes (ducts) that carry milk widen, thicken and become blocked, leading to a fluid build-up. Finally, an infection in the breast can cause a discharge – this would also cause pain and tenderness.

MORE ON p. 174

Because nipple discharge isn't common in teens if you haven't been pregnant, it's always a good idea to have it diagnosed properly by your GP.

MORE ON p. 141

If you have experienced pregnancy, it could be milk – even if the pregnancy was a long time ago.

> I was doing a breast check to check for lumps, and as I was doing it, this milk was dripping out. It led to a whole series of checks. The doctors immediately thought it could be something serious, and I had to get scans and stuff, but it turned out to be normal! They figured it might have just been a little bit of milk leftover in my breasts, just sitting there – from two years earlier! *Nadia*

Boy boobs that won't go away

> We haven't been formally taught about male breasts. *Yash, 16*

> They never went down again. I'm 39 now and they've been there since puberty – my weight's been up and down, I'm addicted to cycling now and I'm keen on fitness, and really lean, and even still the breasts are there. I can't seem to move them. *Keith*

More than fifty per cent of boys going through puberty will have some boob development, most of it mild and barely noticeable. Almost ninety percent of these puberty boy boobs will go away after anywhere between six months and two years. In a small proportion of boys, the boobs remain and don't go away in adulthood. Some men can be quite accepting of this and others can feel distressed. They might worry about their appearance or perhaps wonder why this is happening. If you have boob development that's worrying you for any reason, you can ask your doctor for advice. They can talk to you about what you can expect from just sitting tight and waiting, dealing with how puberty boobs are affecting you emotionally, and also about medication or even surgery. If you're comfortable waiting it out, great! However, if puberty boobs have not gone away after two years, it's advisable to get a check-up.

MORE ON p. 141

> Boys get insecure about their bodies – I know my male friends do. It's not something to brush off or forget about. *Lily, 17*

At home it was a free-for-all, I was constantly body-shamed by both parents and my sibling. My sister was encouraged to call me various names – her favourite, which brought my mother the most laughs, was 'tittie-rama'. Probably a great name for a burlesque show or a topless Bananarama cover band, but not a great name for a young boy going through body-image issues aged 10 to 14. *Mark*

A few years ago, I got back into training and cycling again and of course the weight fell off but I still had them, they're still there. I found out at the start of this year I have diabetes, and so I've actually dropped a whole heap more weight again and probably am at my thinnest since I was 16. They are still there. I've just come to accept them now. There is absolutely no shame in who you are or what you look like. *Dan*

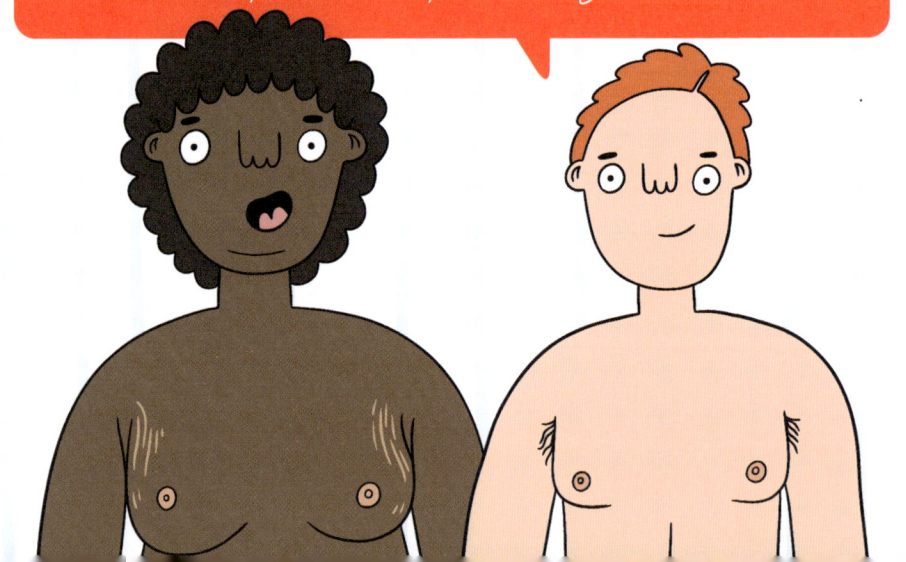

CHANGING MY BOOBS

Over 23 years of reading questions sent to the teen magazine column Dolly Doctor, there were many about whether you could change your boobs. I don't remember ever seeing a question about, say, changing one's shoe size. *Dr Melissa*

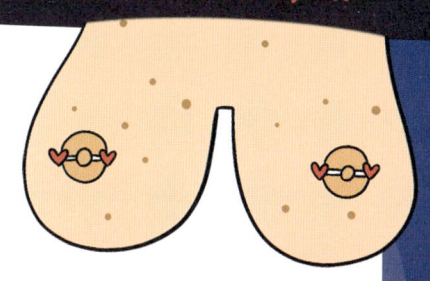

Here are some things people might do to physically change their boobs. Unless you're trans or gender-diverse, it's generally recommended that you wait until your boobs are fully grown before you change them.

Nipple piercing

Nipple piercings can go through just the nipple (the pointy bit that sticks out in most people) or the nipple and part of the areola. Like any piercing, it's best done by a professional piercer using sterile equipment. Healing takes six to eight weeks, which is slightly longer than ear piercings. People like nipple piercings because of how they look, and for some people they enhance sensitivity, making them more erogenous. For others, a piercing can dull sensation.

> It was super painful! I've had lips and tongues and navels pierced and the nipple was by far the most painful – like a nine out of ten for pain! It was a stainless-steel barbell and I reckon it hurt for a good few months. *Laura*

> My cat ripped my nipple ring out. Clean out. I was in shock. I didn't scream but I have the scar to prove it happened! *Ali*

Some of the issues pierced nipples cause include infection of the nipple or breast tissue. In some instances, having a nipple piercing can reduce the amount of breastmilk produced. Nipple piercings usually don't interfere with breastfeeding but for the safety of the baby you need to remove the jewellery.

Breast implants

Getting breast implants, or breast augmentation, is a surgical procedure that can change the shape of your boobs or make your boobs look bigger.

The breast implants themselves are little sacs made from a type of plastic called silicone. The sacs are filled with either sterile saline (salt + water) or more silicone. They come in different shapes and sizes, and are surgically put inside the chest where your breast tissue sits.

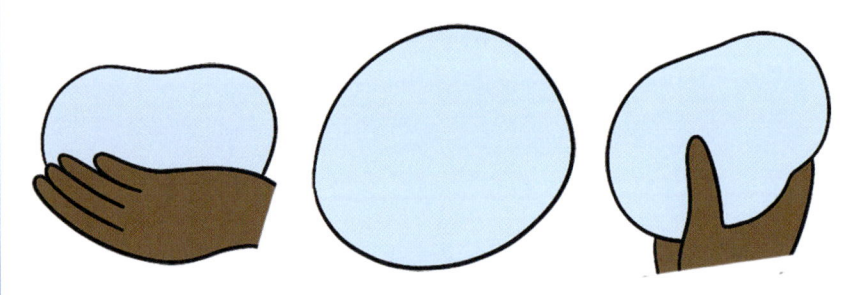

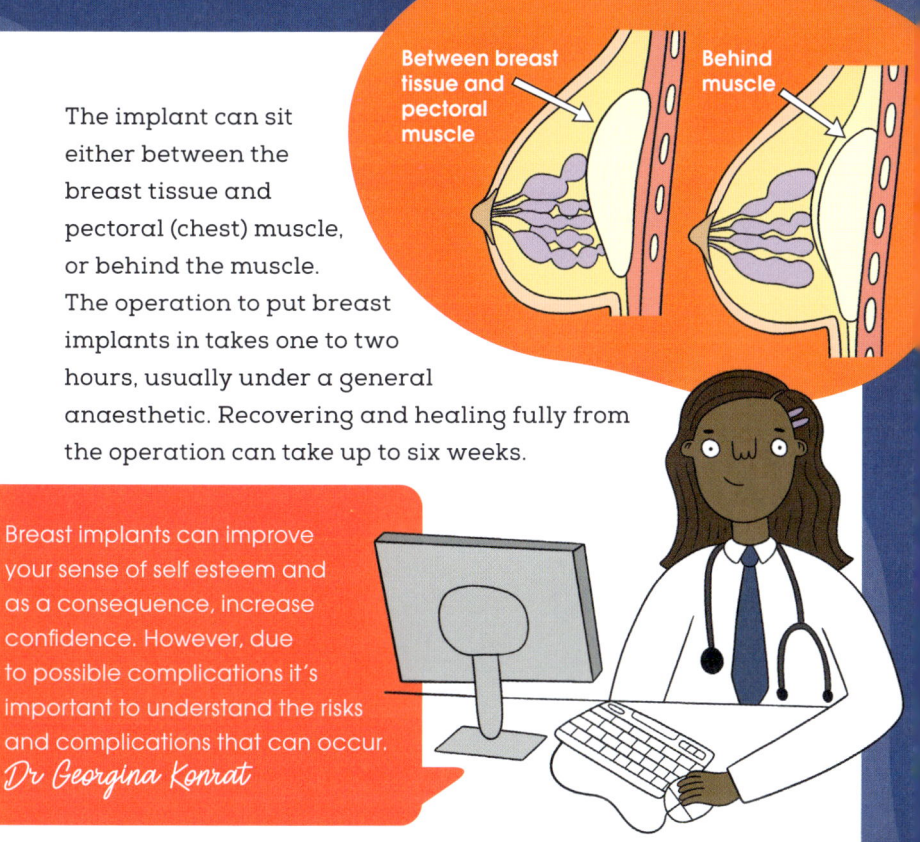

The implant can sit either between the breast tissue and pectoral (chest) muscle, or behind the muscle. The operation to put breast implants in takes one to two hours, usually under a general anaesthetic. Recovering and healing fully from the operation can take up to six weeks.

Between breast tissue and pectoral muscle

Behind muscle

> Breast implants can improve your sense of self esteem and as a consequence, increase confidence. However, due to possible complications it's important to understand the risks and complications that can occur.
> *Dr Georgina Konrat*

Getting implants isn't the end of the process. Breast implants are not considered lifetime devices, and the longer people have them, the greater the chances are that they will develop complications, some of which will require more surgery. Breast implants need to be changed every ten to fifteen years, which involves surgery and likely some scarring. Many women who have had breast implants ultimately need a breast implant revision procedure.

These procedures include:

- **Removing the implants and replacing them with new implants**
- **Repositioning the existing implants**
- **Removing the breast implants without replacement.**

> 22nd of July
> ♥ Change Implant
> ♥ Feed Cat
> ♥ Call Mum

Breast augmentation surgery comes with other risks, too. Some breast implants were found to cause a rare form of cancer around the sac itself. For this reason, some brands of breast implants have been banned. One potential side effect is loss or change of sensation in the nipple. Another is hardening of the breast tissue around the implant. It can occur in the tissue surrounding one or both implants. There is also a small chance that breast implants can interfere with breastfeeding.

> You should never be steamrolled. Or have anyone be patronizing to you, or not have the time to show you photos. I tell all my patients they should get at least one other consultation. No matter how convinced they are (that they want breast implants).
> *Dr Georgina Konrat*

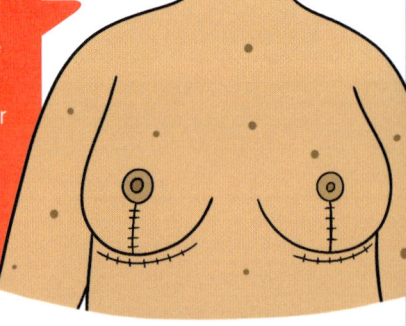

They encapsulated – formed scar tissue around the implant and went really, really hard. Physically, they looked fine. But they felt like hard blocks of cement on my chest. I lived with that for nearly twenty years. I'm asexual so I don't have partners, but when I gave my friends a hug they'd be like, "OH MY GOD, your tits are hard!" And sometimes I'd take advantage of that by giving them an extra-tight squeeze and they'd go, "OH MY GOD, YOU'RE HURTING ME!" *Peta Friend, founder of Trans Pride Australia*

JESSICA'S EXPERIENCE

Looking back, I realize I had low self-esteem.

I'd been to a plastic surgery place and went back for another free consultation. The doctor said, "This is what we discussed last time; if you want, we can do the procedure in two weeks' time." I was like, "YES."

They talked about potential risks – that it is a major surgery, the risk of infection, necrosis (tissue dying), no strenuous activity, how to care for your scar. I don't think they talked about increased cancer risks. He said it was a lifetime thing – he didn't say I would probably need a secondary surgery, or that I'd probably need to change the implants.

My mum said it made her sad that I wanted to change the way I look and that I would spend so much money! So I didn't tell my family.

I was excited and nervous on the day of the surgery. It was all very quick! I had it done and then woke up in recovery really sore and groggy with these giant, tight boobs.

I felt really shitty and was in pain for a week. Getting back into the gym and running took about six weeks.

Because I'd had a lift as well as implants, there was a scar around the nipple and down the middle of the boob. It didn't look good. They were scarred and bloody and bruised. It was two weeks before I could take the tape off – and I had to get them to do it.

Once everything had settled down I was happy with them. I felt like I was strong to get through it.

You have to wear a surgical bra for three months and you can't go swimming. By the time I could wear normal clothes, I was really excited. I felt way more confident with what I could wear and do than I did before.

I haven't lost sensation in my breasts or nipples.

The main difference is how people treat you when you have bosoms and a cleavage. People think that if I look a certain way, I can't be smart or professional. You can be one way or the other – a fake-titted bimbo or smart and unattractive! Some of my old work colleagues – mostly blokes – stalked my socials and gossiped behind my back about my implants.

I went home for Christmas and my mum said, 'I think you really look lovely. It's your body and your money, you can decide what you want to do. I just didn't want you to feel pressured to change the way you look.' That acceptance meant a lot.

This was about three years ago (I'm 30 now). I feel like the novelty has worn off. I'm probably more conservative now with how I dress. Back then I was single and the clothes I wore showed my implants off. Now I have a long-term boyfriend.

I don't regret it. But I don't know if I'd do it again. I put myself through a lot. It was full-on.

DR SAHAR – COSMETIC SURGEON

A lot of ads for cosmetic surgery make it look very easy. But it's actually a huge risk. People have died just from the anaesthetic. You really do need to think about it. I would say to anyone thinking about getting a procedure done, 'Make sure you're informed.' I would emphasize the risks.

There are some cases where surgery might make sense: tubular breasts, uneven breasts, cases where someone's boobs have a psychological impact on them.

Breast surgeries carry risks of infections and scar tissue and take three months to heal properly.

Once you get implants, you will probably need another surgery down the road and people don't often realize that. You might fall pregnant, lose or gain weight, and then they don't look right anymore and you have to change them.

I think the newer generation aren't really into fake boobs. It's not trendy anymore.

Would I want my sister or daughter having augmentation surgery? No.

Breast reduction

Breast reduction mammoplasty is a surgical operation that removes breast tissue to reduce boob size. It can be done both for appearance and to reduce discomfort if the boobs are very large. The operation usually cuts out breast tissue, fat and skin. This operation is done under a general anaesthetic and takes two to five hours.

SONJA'S EXPERIENCE

Since I was about thirteen I've had to alter clothes because of the size of my boobs. I was sixteen when I first raised the idea of a reduction. I went to a doctor, who said to wait until I was eighteen. At eighteen I didn't go back, mainly because I couldn't afford it. And Mum and Dad didn't think I needed it.

The desire for a reduction never went away. I wore a sports bra and crop top just to contain the boobs – stop bounce, flatten them a bit. I got press-studs added to my shirts because they would burst open or gape.

By thirty four, I had enough money – and I'd had enough of being unhappy. They were just TOO BIG. They got in the way.

Once I decided, I went with Mum to see what the surgeon would say. That was very scary. And confronting and vulnerable. I had to show him my breasts. It's like exposing your most embarrassing secret. Nothing was forced and he chatted about what was appropriate, what he could do. I went away and thought about it but I had pretty much made up my mind to do it! I was ready.

Before the surgery I was nervous. I still wanted to feel like me and I wasn't sure if I was going to. I was nervous that they might get it wrong, or they'd be uneven, and then I'd be worse off.

It's a really big surgery and a really painful recovery. You think it's an easy thing but it wasn't. I think you can be warned, but until you're in it you don't realize how painful it is.

In breast reduction surgery they open you up in an anchor shape – from your areola down, then left and right. That's three scars, and if you have quite large breasts that's a lot of cutting, plus the removal of breast tissue, the internal stitching of the tissue inside, and then the skin – and because they removed so much, they moved my areola as well. It's quite full-on – not at all like a breast implant.

When you wake up, you're totally strapped up. Can't move too much. Even lying down hurt. I did not expect that amount of pain. I needed Mum with me that whole week. She had to help me move – I couldn't roll onto my side or get out of bed properly, I needed help putting clothes on. That was the worst part. But when it all had settled? THE RELIEF. It's the best thing I've ever done!

After a week I went back to the doctor. When he took the bandages off, it was like all my prayers had been answered. They were smaller. Lighter. And much perkier. It felt good. I felt much more comfortable in my skin. There were so many things that came with it – I could wear clothes that I didn't have to adjust. I could wear just one normal bra as opposed to a sports bra and a crop top. The back pain went. And I could wear a sexy bra! I had never worn a strapless bra.

The first time I went out, it was like an 'outing' – an internal outing of myself! I didn't tell anyone but my mum and my two best friends about the surgery. So it was an outing just for me – and no-one noticed that I'd had the reduction!

I was single at the time and I'm glad about that. It was TOTALLY EXCITING to be going out. It was like a new chapter. I didn't realise how much it was affecting me, having these large breasts that I wasn't happy with.

My only regret is I wish I had got it done sooner. I felt good that I only had it done for ME. And I wasn't trying to impress anybody. F***, IT FELT GREAT. I'm never looking back.

In males, breast reduction surgery is usually to treat gynecomastia. This is when puberty has passed, and the person might be quite lean, but breast tissue remains. The man might have liposuction surgery, which removes breast fat but not the breast gland tissue itself. Or he might have a mastectomy, which removes the breast gland tissue. Sometimes a combination of both surgeries is done.

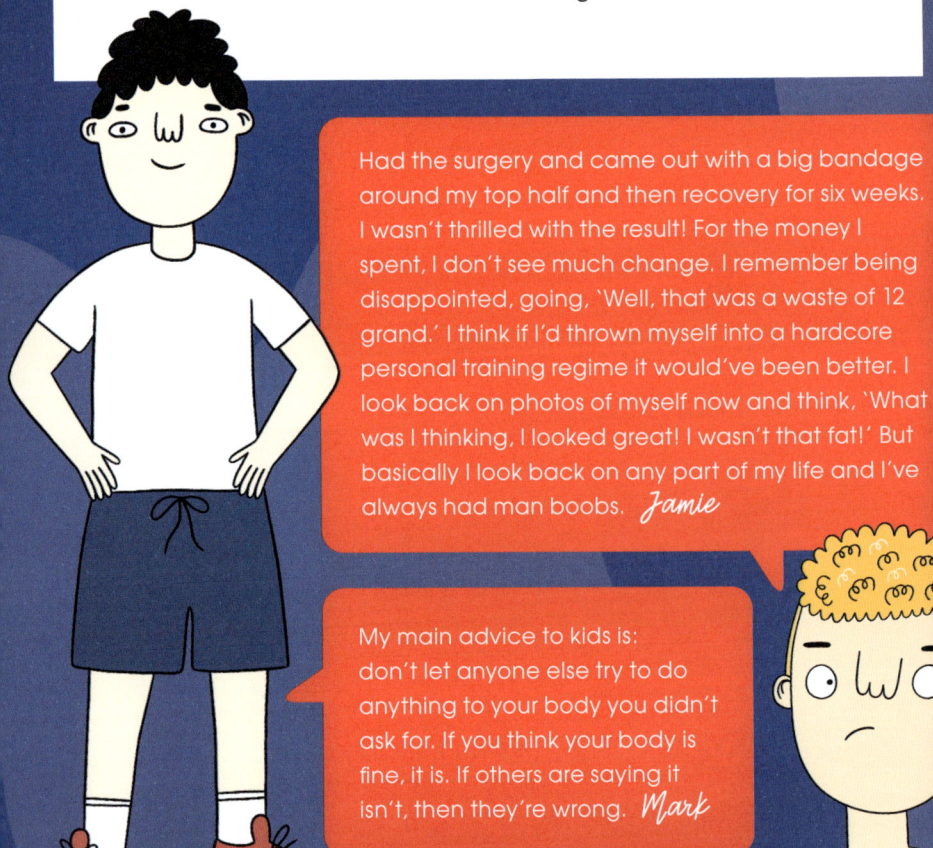

Had the surgery and came out with a big bandage around my top half and then recovery for six weeks. I wasn't thrilled with the result! For the money I spent, I don't see much change. I remember being disappointed, going, 'Well, that was a waste of 12 grand.' I think if I'd thrown myself into a hardcore personal training regime it would've been better. I look back on photos of myself now and think, 'What was I thinking, I looked great! I wasn't that fat!' But basically I look back on any part of my life and I've always had man boobs. *Jamie*

My main advice to kids is: don't let anyone else try to do anything to your body you didn't ask for. If you think your body is fine, it is. If others are saying it isn't, then they're wrong. *Mark*

Gender identity and boobs

A trans girl may wish to grow boobs whereas a trans boy may wish the opposite. Other gender-diverse teens may be comfortable with having or not having boobs, but might wish to change other physical characteristics (such as the amount of body hair).

As we keep saying in this book, everyone's experience of boobs is different! It's all part of the wonderful diversity in humans in every culture all over the world.

> I didn't know that I was trans until halfway through high school so I didn't make the connection between boobs and gender. So that didn't really bother me – it wasn't dysphoria, it was more shame because I was an early developer and when you're in primary school kids point out things, like, 'You've got boobs!' *Skylar, 23*

> Hmmm, they look how I feel.

Binding my boobs

Binding – tightly wrapping fabric around your chest – is something people can do when they want their chest to appear flatter. Binding is worn underneath clothes.

PEOPLE HAVE USED ALL SORTS OF METHODS TO BIND THEIR CHESTS OVER THE CENTURIES. THESE DAYS THERE ARE GUIDELINES TO MAKE SURE BINDING IS SAFE.

Binding that is too tight or uses inappropriate fabrics can cause damage to the skin or ribs and make breathing difficult. There are now plenty of binders available that tick the boxes for safety and comfort. They are made of breathable material and come in a range of sizes, lengths and styles.

Binders should not be too small or tight, should not be left on for more than six to eight hours straight and should not be worn to sleep in at night. Big no-nos include tape or other adhesives, and non-breathable fabric that can damage skin. Firm sports bras are also sometimes used instead of chest binders.

If you want to get more advice about safe binding practices, this site has heaps of information:
point5cc.com/binding-101-tips-to-bind-your-chest-safely/

You could also look at the Gender GP website:
gendergp.com

GC2B UK and Spectrum Outfitters are great companies created by trans guys that make high-quality binders that are super comfy and safe.
GC2B:
gc2b.co
Spectrum Outfitters:
spectrumoutfitters.co.uk

WYATT'S EXPERIENCE

I'm 18 and I hit puberty in Year Six. I got quite a big chest from a young age, and I had back pain and was like, 'This is a curse! I don't want these here!' It was a muddle of confusion and sadness. A very weird time.

I tried to be accepting of my boobs. I had a super-super-girly phase and would only wear feminine things. It was a bit of a denial phase – I was attempting to fit in.

When I first started binding I used really small sports bras, and I would cut up old tights and stack them in the fashion of a binder – no-one should ever do that! But I had double-Ds as a 14-year-old and didn't have access to (commercially made) binders. I was young and not out. I was binding dangerously. I was in more pain with my chest than before, but there was this euphoria! It was like, 'This makes more sense to me now!' I got my first proper binder around 16 and it was like INSTANT RELIEF. It just does the job with one piece of fabric! Binders from reputable sources are made safely so you can wear them for an extended period of time without any damage.

I'm nearly two years on testosterone and probably three months away from top (chest) surgery. My body's more comfortable to me now. Only people I trust see me without a binder and they're not going to perceive me as not a man just because I've got boobs.

To a younger kid who feels the same, I want to say: the uncomfortable feeling won't last forever! Dysphoria is sadly a part of being trans, but it will lessen. The beautiful thing about being a young queer person is YOU CHOOSE who you want to be around, you CHOOSE your friends and family, and you get to a place where you're not so worried about everything.

I'm SO HAPPY with my life, with the people in my life, the people I love who have validated my identity.

Stopping my boobs from growing

MORE ON p. 10

Trans boys identify as male, but puberty will bring on boob development (and, later on, periods). Trans boys can take hormone medication that will put a pause on puberty. In the UK all people seeking the use of hormone blockers undergo an in-depth clinical review with the NHS Gender Identity Development Service (GIDS). Where a patient is under sixteen, and they, their parent(s) or carer, and clinicians believe that hormone blocking treatment may be appropriate, the GIDS decision-making process will be reviewed by an independent Multi-Professional Review Group.

Removing my boobs – 'top surgery'

Trans boys and men might reach a time when they would like to physically, permanently have their boobs removed. This involves an operation under a general anaesthetic. In the UK, it's not possible to get top surgery if you're under the age of eighteen. However, you can definitely seek advice from doctors and surgeons about what's involved.

Trans boobs

Trans girls reach puberty and may wish to stop the growth of facial and body hair, muscle bulking and genital changes. Like trans boys, hormone medication to 'block' puberty can be taken at the earliest stages of puberty as a temporary measure.

> When you first start taking hormones and your body starts developing in a way that you see yourself, it's like going through a second puberty. But it's one that's very much controlled by you. I remember (when I was on hormones), every morning I would get out of bed and I would look. I would look at myself in the mirror. Looking for the physical manifestation of my gender! The main thing was breast development – it happened within three months. *Peta Friend, founder of Trans Pride Australia*

Trans girls may also wish to have a more female body shape. Some trans girls wear special bras that have space for an insert, which can be made of silicon or simply be a small, spongy cushion. Sometimes they want to start growing boobs. To do this, they can be prescribed gender affirming hormones, which are hormones that make boobs grow. From the age of 16, teenagers who've been on hormone blockers for at least 12 months may be given cross-sex hormones, also known as gender-affirming hormones, as the law presumes they are able to give informed consent.

GENDER SERVICES

Services for people with questions and concerns about gender are available in the UK and Ireland. They are staffed with trained professionals who understand the unique challenges faced by gender-diverse people. The Gender Identity Development Service (GIDS) is an NHS health clinic specialising in working with children with gender identity issues.

They aim to provide help to young people (and their families) experiencing any difficulties in relation to their gender identity, working closely together as a group of professionals from different backgrounds, including clinical psychologists, social workers and paediatric endocrinology.

After a referral, patients are assessed to determine the tailored care they and their family may need. They provide ongoing therapy and support groups for young people and their families to safely explore their own feelings, to normalise gender variance, to have access to role-models and to both offer and receive support from other families.

When I was able to look at my chest for the first time (after my top surgery), there was still so much swelling it didn't look any different. But when the swelling finally went down, it felt ... correct. When your body looks how it should, there's a feeling of things being correct. Not having to wear a binder and being treated as a cis male by strangers was how I knew I was right. *Skylar, 23*

I was 23 when I started to affirm my gender. I still like to say 'transition' – because I do think about it as a transition, because you are going from one place to another – but 'affirming your gender' is a more positive way to say it, like, 'I was always this gender, I'm just making it real.'

It was a great experience. The hormones took over and started in my body straight away. Little breast buds started to grow. My boobs started to form and it was really painful when they were growing! My boobs didn't grow as big as I wanted, so I got implants in 2015 and that was a life-changing experience. They're part of my identity. I take good care of them. I feel like I couldn't live without them. *Victoria Anthony, 30*

GRACE'S EXPERIENCE

I'm 20. When I was 12 I had a 'light-bulb moment' and knew I was trans. I came out then. At 13 I started testosterone blockers and at 15 I started oestrogen.

I used to be very thin and I gained some weight and my shape changed on the oestrogen. I am a B or a C cup, and the oestrogen also made my hips grow. This made me more confident. I felt legitimate – these body changes were self-actualising for me.

Body image is a big topic for trans people. There is no one way to transition (from one gender to another), but transition has the purpose of reducing dysphoria when your body does not fit your gender identity. Everyone experiences dysphoria differently. I had terrible body image when I was young, I felt like I was in purgatory.

If I had one message about body image now, it would be that our body is ours alone. It's not for men to objectify or think they own. For me, taking hormones gave me confidence about who I am. Being able to love myself came with having that confidence about my body.

REST-OF-YOUR-LIFE BOOBS

What happens to boobs in pregnancy

Entire books have been written about pregnancy and breastfeeding. We're assuming this is probably a while off for you, so we're not going to try to cover EVERYTHING here, but we do want to communicate the basics, because they're super interesting! *(You might need to know this stuff in the future, or maybe you won't!)*

Sometimes the first clue a person has that they are pregnant is a change in their boobs. Their boobs feel different – often super tender and ouchy, or the nipples feel sensitive. During pregnancy, milk-making preparation goes into overdrive and everything swells up – a little, or a lot – maybe even by three cup sizes! Nipples get plump and ready to be suckled. The areolae and nipples darken in colour, and those little lumps in the areolae that make moisturiser might also swell up.

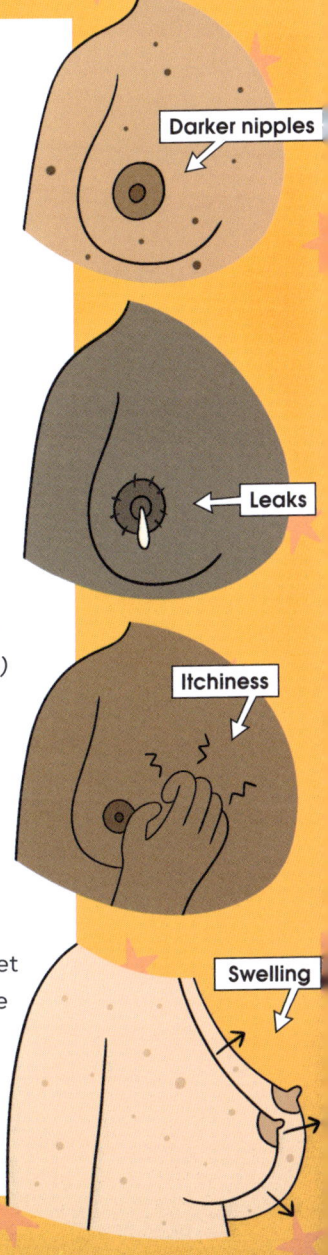

MORE ON p. 63

Darker nipples

Leaks

Itchiness

Swelling

> After having children, they're amazing! I was completely flat my entire life and I used to sit there and PRAY for boobs! I was really skinny, which is why I had no chest! Then I had children and have a D-cup now. They're big and they stayed big – maybe a bit saggier, but they're good. *Nadia*

Breastfeeding

When a pregnancy finishes, hormone signals are sent up to the brain and then down to the boobs to switch on milk production. For the first three or four days, a small amount of clear or yellowish liquid comes out of the nipples. It doesn't look like milk and you might think it rather insignificant, but to a new baby it's liquid gold. This special milk is called colostrum and, though there's only a few teaspoons of it made a day, it's magical stuff full of ingredients that protect a baby from infection. It also boosts their immune system.

After about three days breast milk 'comes in'. This just means that boobs swell up with milk and when nipples are suckled by a baby (or, in some situations, by using a breast pump) milk flows out in much bigger volumes (on average about 400ml per day). Milk production in boobs keeps adjusting for up to two weeks after a baby is born and then reaches steady production of anywhere between 500ml and 1L per day. By this stage breast milk contains a balance of nutrients that will help the baby grow over the next several months.

Boobs make milk no matter which way a pregnancy finishes – giving birth to a baby, having a miscarriage or having a termination (abortion). For milk to keep being made, nipples need to be regularly suckled or stimulated. If this doesn't happen, boobs will shut down milk production automatically, but it can take several days or even a couple of weeks. Sometimes doctors will prescribe medication to help stop milk production more quickly.

Breasts are designed to breastfeed, but it's still a skill that needs to be learned, and some people find it difficult. There are special practitioners called 'lactation consultants' who can help teach people how to breastfeed their babies.

> I literally felt like my son was sucking the boobs out of me. Afterwards, my boobs felt smaller and they dropped a bit. *Claire, 40*

My boobs were such a source of attention – sexual and otherwise – for such a long time. Then, weirdly, they let me down – I'm a twice-failed breastfeeder. I was so devo. When I couldn't breastfeed I sat on a pump for EIGHT MONTHS!! Six times a day for eight months. With my second kid I pumped for two months and decided that was enough. *Nelly, 46*

Send down the milk

Because I had big boobs I thought breastfeeding would come naturally – but it didn't, and milk production didn't come naturally either. *Bernadette*

CONTAINS: MILK

Breastfeeding was quite affirming for me because I've always been very flat-chested, and when I realised they would still feed my babies, I started to see my boobs for what they were: perfectly acceptable! *Kim*

Breast cancer

Anyone with breast tissue can hypothetically get breast cancer. That includes women, men, trans and gender-diverse people. The good news is, it's extremely rare in young people and almost unheard of in teenagers. Breast cancer happens when the genetic material inside some breast-tissue cells mutates. It gets reprogrammed, telling the cells to multiply, and they do so in an out-of-control way.

> Girls and women are taught to check their breasts and I had been brought up with that message, so I did check my breasts and when I felt the lump I immediately thought I had breast cancer and got very frightened and saw a doctor the next day. *Valasca*

We hear about breast cancer a lot because it is the most common cancer affecting women in the UK. About 55,000 women and 370 men are diagnosed with breast cancer every year. There isn't just one type of breast cancer – everyone diagnosed with it has to have a personalised assessment to figure out which cells in the breast tissue have become cancerous. The cells which form the lobules and those which form the tubes (ducts) are the cell types most commonly associated with breast cancer. When someone is diagnosed with breast cancer, the

> My body acceptance and my self-confidence in my body actually improved because of my breast cancer. I've had lots of good things come out of it! I still wouldn't recommend it though! *Valasca*

doctors also figure out whether the proliferation of those cells has spread further into, and outside of, the breast. That's why treatment for breast cancer varies a lot – it might involve surgery to remove the cancer lump, or the whole breast (see mastectomy, below). It might involve chemotherapy or radiotherapy to kill off the cancerous cells and stop them from multiplying.

We know much more about breast cancer now than we did even a few years ago, which means many more people survive it than in the past. It's recommended that women (without any lumps or breast issues) between the ages of fifty and seventy-four get mammograms every two years.

There's no known specific cause for breast cancer. But we know that some things can increase your risk of breast cancer, including being female, getting older, genetics, obesity, alcohol and smoking.

Mastectomy

Mastectomy is surgery to remove all tissue from a breast, most commonly as a way to treat or prevent breast cancer. It's a pretty serious procedure that requires a general anaesthetic and taking around six weeks off work. After mastectomy some people choose to have breast reconstruction surgery with a breast implant, but others prefer to leave the breast flat. The reconstruction surgery might happen at the same time as the mastectomy, or sometime later (weeks, months or longer).

When I woke up I couldn't look at it. For a long time. So in my mind I still had both breasts. And I didn't have a breast for more than a year but in that time I still went on online dating and met some really nice guys who didn't care that I only had one boob. And that was a really good experience for me – learning that there's plenty of people out there who will love you for who you are and whether you've got one boob or five boobs is no big deal for them. *Valasca*

I took my best friend along to the last consultation and I remember going, "Take them both off," and my friend saying, "Are you sure?" And Cyndi (the surgeon) interrupted her and said, "She's sure." They would have had to cut through my abs to build new boobs and that felt like a Frankenstein's experiment to me – building a fake body just to fit the stereotype of what a woman's body looks like – and it really enraged me. I've never regretted that decision – ever. And I love having a flat chest – I love it! *Vicki*

LISA'S EXPERIENCE

In our mid-forties my friend Tash told me that in the women's section of David Jones department store, there's a little section (the Rose Clinic) where you can get a mammogram! So I went and had the bejesus squeezed out of my boob. Two weeks later they asked me to return and I had to get a biopsy in both boobs! That really hurt and the nurse held my hand and I cried.

I took one of my best mates to the follow-up appointment. I was so scared. She held my hand as the doctor said they had found not a lump but a small cluster of micro-calcifications. Two weeks later I had hookwire day surgery to remove the cluster. Pretty simple procedure – but I was bandaged up for a week. Now I have a three-centimetre scar around my nipple. I have learned to live with it and it reminds me that it could've been much worse!

Wrinkly boobs, old boobs

As you get older, hormonal changes in your body will make your boobs change. Like the skin on other parts of your body, the skin on your boobs will wrinkle. The areola tends to become smaller and may nearly disappear. Breast tissue becomes less glandular and more fatty after you turn forty, which makes them feel less firm and full. Your breasts get smaller, sometimes by a cup size or more (unless you put on weight, in which case they may get bigger). As the years go by, you might also notice a wider space between your breasts. Declining oestrogen levels during and after menopause make breast tissue dehydrated and less elastic, so your breasts lose their once-rounded shape and begin to sag.

NONE OF THIS IS BAD – OR GOOD. IT'S JUST LIFE!

Yes, now I have wrinkly boobs!
Nelly, 46

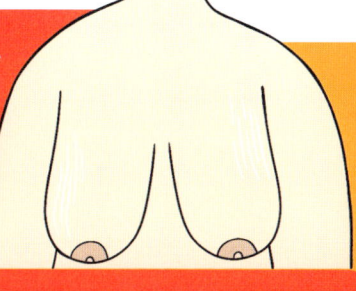

I think my boobs are still in good shape at this age! No wrinkles. My boobs aren't very big – sort of standard size – and I have always had very good skin. But I have noticed that my nipples are very small compared with other girls'. I didn't notice very much change in my boobs! I'm not proud, there's nobody to look at them. My own mother shrank quite a lot – she was middle-aged when the war hit Japan and they didn't have enough food. Her whole body shrank, became small. That might make a difference in the shape and function of the boobs. They looked kind of like a squashed grape! When I went to the public bath, lots of old ladies had no fat in their boobs! They looked just like an osembe – or biscuit! *Yoshiko (Yumi's mum), 77*

BOOB *Pledge*

'I HEREBY SWEAR ...

That **MY BOOBS** are mine – they're for me, and not for anyone else!

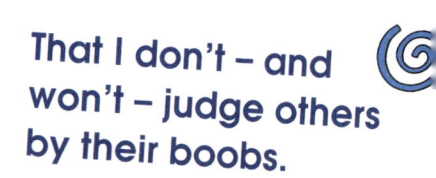

That I don't – and won't – judge others by their boobs.

That I'm allowed to do whatever I want with my boobs – whether that's showing them off, hiding them away, sharing them with someone, wearing no bra or painting them purple! The thing I'm NOT allowed to do is make other people feel bad for whatever they have – or don't have – up front.

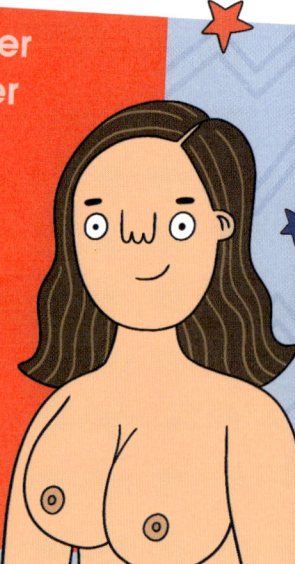

ALTHOUGH IT'S TEMPTING, I PLEDGE TO TRY NOT TO COMPARE MY BOOBS TO OTHER PEOPLE'S BOOBS!

To internalise the truth that there is no such thing as 'perfect' – there's just what I have. Accepting myself as wonderful, as whole and complete, is part of my life's work. And it starts now – when I look in the mirror and I say, "Hey, friend. You're all right, y'know? I like you."

I accept **OTHERS** and their boobs.

And, therefore, I accept myself and **MY** boobs.

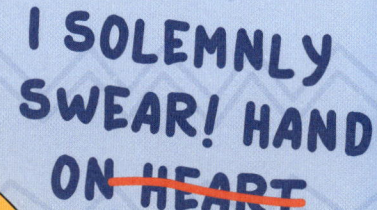

I SOLEMNLY SWEAR! HAND ON ~~HEART~~ BOOB.'

GLOSSARY

GENDER DYSPHORIA
This is when a person feels distressed because their gender identity does not match the sex they were presumed to be when they were born.

AREOLA
The plural is 'areolae'. The circle of skin and tissue around the nipple. The areola and nipple together are usually a darker colour than the skin on the rest of the breast.

GLAND
An organ in the body that makes a specific substance. For example, sweat glands make sweat and salivary glands make saliva. Some glands in the breast make milk. Some glands in the body make hormones.

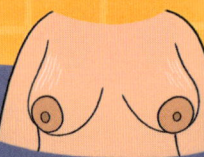

BINDER
Usually a piece of clothing made to fit around the chest to compress boobs. It creates a flatter appearance of the chest.

HORMONE
A chemical messenger that travels through our blood until it reaches its designated stop or stops. It then directs cells and tissues to grow, change or perform a special function.

CHROMOSOME
Part of the genetic material inside our cells. Chromosomes are made up of genes, which are pre-programmed to make our bodies (and brains) grow or appear in specific ways (such as final height, eye colour, or the appearance of genitals and boobs).

MAMMOGRAM
An X-ray of the breast(s).

GENDER
A person's sense of being female, male or something else. There's more to human beings than each person only being either a 'girl' or a 'boy' – some people are somewhere in between, both or neither.

MAMMOPLASTY
An operation that aims to change the size or shape of breasts. A reduction mammoplasty removes some (but not all) breast tissue, usually to reduce the size of breasts.

MASTECTOMY

An operation that removes all breast tissue (including the nipple and areola).

PROGESTERONE

Another hormone involved in breast development during puberty, and the menstrual cycle.

MENSTRUAL CYCLE

What happens between the start of one menstrual period (aka 'period') and the next. The menstrual hormones are super busy during the cycle – they thicken the lining of the uterus while ripening an egg inside one of the ovaries, then they make the egg pop out (aka 'ovulate') and then, if there is no fertilisation (pregnancy), the hormones prepare the uterus to shed its lining, which is what comes out as a period. These hormones can have an effect on boob tissue, too, which is why some people have swollen or tender boobs just before a period. A menstrual cycle takes on average 28 days, but can be anywhere from around 22 to 45 days in teens!

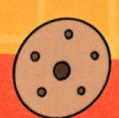

SEX

The word 'sex' can have a lot of meanings. Sometimes it refers to a person's chromosomes, reproductive organs and physical characteristics that fall across a spectrum from female to male. Sex also means activities a person does, either alone or with someone else, that are physically intimate or sexually stimulating. It can include: kissing; online interacting such as sexy talk; looking, touching or rubbing together parts of the body that are sexually sensitive, such as genitals; or having intercourse, just to name a few.

NON-BINARY

When a person does not identify as either female or male.

SEXISM

Discrimination against someone because of their sex or gender.

OESTROGEN

One of the hormones that makes breasts grow. It does a lot of other things to the body too, especially in relation to the menstrual cycle.

TRANSGENDER

When a person identifies as the gender that doesn't match the sex they were presumed to be at birth.

MORE RESOURCES

Call

CHILDLINE .... 0800 111 / 0800 66 66 66
PROUD TRUST 0161 660 3347
SAMARITANS 116 123

Learn

Breast Cancer UK

TransgenderTeenSurvivalGuide

The Mix

Stonewall

Brook

nhs.uk/conditions/gender-dysphoria/treatment/

Support

againstbreastcancer.org.uk

Ask

supportline.org.uk
gendergp.com

mermaidsuk.org.uk
gids.nhs.uk

Buy

BINDERS

Spectrum Outfitters

Gc2b UK

Underworks

BRAS

Boody.co.uk

Cottonon.com

Bravissimo

H&M

Marks & Spencer

ACKNOWLEDGEMENTS

This book is dedicated to Donna, whose smile is as big as the sky. I'm so grateful to Yumi, who trusted in our collaborative and creative potential. Your intellect, energy and sheer sass are amazing. It's been a fun, hectic and immensely fulfilling journey!

Team Hardie Grant Children's Publishing are awesome to work with – a huge thank you to Marisa Pintado, Pooja Desai, Luna Soo and Pen White. To Jennifer Latham – your talent, intuition and dedication to this audience are incredible, thank you again for sharing them with us and bringing our words to life. Thank you to Benython Oldfield from Zeitgeist Agency for all your support.

This book could not be what it is without the wisdom so generously shared with me by these incredible colleagues and experts: Cristyn Davies (ambassador for Twenty10), Dr Annabelle Hobbs, Associate Professor Michelle Telfer, Dr Lisa Tan, Professor Kate Steinbeck and Terence Humphreys (Co-Executive Director, Twenty10). Thank you so much to the young people who contributed to and reviewed sections of the book – you know who you are.

Thank you to Mitchell, for sharing the journey with me, but more importantly for helping me see what it's like for a dad who had to figure it all out when teendom came along … you're somewhere in this book too, I just haven't told you! My forever people – Hannah-Rose, Georgia, Samantha and Julian – thank you for just being, and some more.

Most of all, I want to thank the thousands of letter-writers to Dolly Doctor and the hundreds of young people who have trusted me with your worries and wonderings over many years. I've learned so much from you.

Dr Melissa

Thank you to my mother, Yoshiko Stynes, who breastfed me for three months from her own body (!) and then spent the rest of my life demonstrating what a gregarious optimist looks like in the wild. Thank you to Anouk for her sincere and bottomless empathy. The laughs we have together are among the greatest in the world. Thank you to Dee Dee for her dogged commitment to learning and achieving – you make me look lazy and how dare you! Thanks, Mercy, for being the embodiment of potential, smarts and power. I'm proud of how few fucks you give. And thanks to Magnus, whose devilish energy and relentless need to make everything hilarious is like the combustion in the putt-putt power of our ship.

Talking about boobs was a gift and a joy for all the women I spoke to – thank you for sharing with such naughtiness and delight. And for the men I spoke to, a source of confusion and some agony. Thank you for being open and generous, and for speaking through your fear.

Dr Melissa, what a wonderful woman to have a career entwined with! Thanks for your forbearance, communication skills and commitment to scientific truth. Jenny Latham, over there on the other side of the world, thank you again for the humour and vision of relatable humans you muster out of thin air. Thank you to Penelope White, Pooja Desai, Luna Soo, Kristy Lund-White and Marisa Pintado at Hardie Grant, and thank you to Benython Oldfield, our book agent.

Thank you to the clusters of friends who've been like life rafts over the past year. I hope me learning how much I treasure even our smallest interactions has made me a better friend to you.

Finally, thank you to my boobs, both left and right. I never thought you were perfect, or pin-up, or enviable, but it turns out you were just right, for me.

Yumi

CONTRIBUTORS

Thank you so much to our wonderful contributors:

Abigail, Alex, Alexandra, Ali, Amy, Andrew, Anouk, Berno, Bianca, Candy, Catharine Lumby, Claire, Clem, Cleo, Cristyn Davies, Dan, Dee Dee, Dr Georgina Konrat, Dr Sahar, Edie, Elaine, Emma-Jayne, Evie, Florence, Grace, Gracie N, Holly, Jamie, JB, Jem, Jessica, Katie, Keith, Kim, Kirri, Laura, Lauren Elise Threadgate, Lily, Linda, Lisa, Lisa, Lisa, Lorna, Louise, Marihuzka, Marisa, Mark, Mary, Miranda, Nadia, Naoko, Nelly, Olive, Peggy, Penny, Peta Friend *(founder of Trans Pride Australia)*, Pooja, Rebekah, Rosie, Skylar, Sonja, Stella Barton, Valasca, Vicki, Victoria Anthony, Wyatt, Yash and Yoshiko.

Your honesty is so appreciated.

ABOUT THE AUTHORS

Yumi Stynes is an Australian broadcaster, writer and co-creator of award-winning podcast *Ladies, We Need To Talk*, which explores tricky topics and taboos around women's health.

Dr Melissa Kang is a practising medical doctor specialising in adolescent health and sexuality, an academic and one of the brains behind the iconic *Dolly Doctor* column in Australia's *Dolly* Magazine.

ABOUT THE ILLUSTRATOR

Jenny Latham is an illustrator from the United Kingdom. Since graduating from Falmouth University in 2019, Jenny has illustrated all three books in the *Welcome to* series. Jenny believes that *Welcome to Your Boobs* will highlight the importance of breast awareness and support young people to understand how we all develop at different stages in our adolescent years. Jenny hopes, through her illustrations, to empower others to speak openly about their bodies and the changes we all experience.